OUR EARLIEST ATTEMPT AT INDEPENDENCE

OUR EARLIEST ATTEMPT AT INDEPENDENCE.

By

BHAI PARMANAND, M. A., M. L. A.

GYAN

Published by

GYAN

Gyan Publishing House
5, Ansari Road
Daryaganj, New Delhi-110002
Phone: 011-47034999, 9811692060
E-mail: books@gyanbooks.com

Distribution Network
gyanbooks.com
India, USA, Canada, UK, Australia, France

ISBN: 978-81-212-7995-6 (PB)
First Published, 1907

2nd Impression 2023

Printed at: Gyan Press, Delhi.

OUR EARLIEST ATTEMPT AT INDEPENDENCE
Author: BHAI PARMANAND

Our Earliest Attempt at Independence

BY

BHAI PARMANAND.

OUR EARLIEST ATTEMPT AT INDEPENDENCE.

BY

BHAI PARMANAND, M. A., M. L. A.

BOOKS READ AND CONSULTED :—

I The Histories of India by James Mill, Elphinstone and Sir William Hunter.

II Orme's Military transactions and Malleson's "Decisive battles of India."

III The Persian History of the period by Ghoolam Hoosein, a contemporary historian.

IV Grant Duff's history of the Mahrattas and Wilke's History of Mysore.

V Lecky's History of England.

VI Burke's Speeches.

VII Gleigh's Memoirs of Hastings.

VIII State Papers by Mr Forrest.

IX A large number of tracts and pamphlets.

X Six reports of the Secret Committees appointed by the English Parliment on Indian affairs.

The principal source of the material are however 264 volumes of the private and official correspondence of Hastings, containing a record of the consultations of the Supreme Council of Calcutta and of the Councils of the other two Presidencies, which are preserved in the British Museum, London.

PREFACE.

The narrative in this volume possesses several distinct features of interest. Few students of history know that the War of American Independence exercised a lasting influence on the development of events in this country. The unity of modern history is perhaps no-where better illustrated than in this inter-action of American and Hindu history. The people of England attempted to impose the colonial system on America and India at the same time. Both in the East and the West, the policy of aggressive Imperialism produced a revolution, which was curative in its character in America and preventive in its aim in India. The American colonists tried to subvert British authority: the Hindus united to prevent its consolidation. The last quarter of the eighteenth century witnessed both the conflicts, which were waged far apart, for the same object. The issue is known to all. America won the fight: and India failed in the attempt. The close connection of the two events is shown by the fact that the news of the surrender of Burgoyne first suggested to Hastings the plan of establishing an Empire in India to make up for the loss of the old dominions. Cornwallis, who left America a sadder and a wiser man at the end of the War, was the pioneer of British rule in India. Imperialism, fleeing from the New world, sought a new field in the old.

The participation of the French in both the struggles adds additional interest to the story and emphasizes the unity of historical causation referred to above.

To students of Indian history, this volume may be useful as a continuation of Mr. Ranade's work on the Rise and growth of the Marhatta Empire. It takes up the thread of events where that gifted author leaves it off. But from the view-point of the country as a whole, its peculiar interest and charm lies in this that the narrative is a detailed description of the earliest combined attempt made by the Princes of India to liberate their country from the impending foreign yoke. Here-in we come across for the first time, how the British policy and plan of the conquest of India is laid bare to these princes and they for once make up their minds to resist it. This combination was not quite sincere or for the common good and led to no success. Their troubles went on and having lost all hope in other ways the princes or their helpless successors sought the aid of the army and created a rising in 1857 which again ended in a great disaster.

It is hoped that this essay may stimulate an intelligent interest in the study of our history. The old order has changed. Time has healed up the old wounds. The last Great War has radically changed the British angle of vision. There are great signs of new hope in the awakening of the people.

Bhai Parmanand.

INTRODUCTORY.

From factories to forts, from forts to garrisons, from garrisons to armies, from armies to conquests, the gradations were natural and the result inevitable; where we could not find a danger, we were determined to find a quarrel."—Philip Francis: Speech on India affairs, *1787*.

The Beginnings.

At the close of the fifteenth and the early part of the sixteenth centuries, two new races appeared in India, which were to mould her future destinies. One of them came from the mountains of the North-West, and the other from the Sea. The former, Muhammadans in religion, came as conquerors; while the latter, Christians by faith, came in the garb of merchants.

The invasion of Baber brought a new dynasty to the throne of Delhi which gave stability to the government of the country and put an end to the interminable revolutions that the country had witnessed ever since the Muhammadan conquest. Baber's descendants were destined to rule over India for nearly three centuries. The establishment of a strong Government under the Moguls put a stop for sometime to the growth of the political influence of the traders from across the Sea.

The long struggle between the Moors and the Christians in the principalities of Spain and Portugal, which resulted in the complete expulsion of the Moors from the Peninsula, had made the two races mortal enemies of each other. Encouraged by their success, the Christians started in pursuit of the Moors along the western coast of the African continent with a determination to destroy their trade which was the source of their prosperity. By the end of the fifteenth century, the Portuguese appeared on the west coast af India. Their first struggles were with the Moors who had established their trade in that part of the country and who did their utmos in keeping out their old enemies. The Portuguese however achieved a fair amount of success in ousting the Moors and gaining for themselves a considerable influence at the courts of the petty Indian Princes. They had complete control of the Eastern trade for nearly a century. During this period they became enormously wealthy and thus excited a feeling of envy among other European nations. Wealth and the luxuries that followed in its train had already corrupted this small and enterprising people, when the annexation of Portugal by Spain in 1580 utterly crushed their spirit. The sea-power of Spain received a death-blow by the failure of Phillip's ill-fated Armada. Maritime supremacy then passed away to the English and to the Dutch who, having thrown off the yoke of Spain, enriched themselves at the expense of the Portuguese colonies which had become Spanish possesions.

East India Company.

It was after a severe clash with the Portuguese that the English succeeded in establishing themselves in 1612 in Surat on the western coast of India from where they gradually extended their settlements to the Eastern coast. In 1644, Dr. Boughton procured from the Emperor Shahjahan special trade concessions for the English who had established their trade in Bengal. Bengal, being the richest province and famous for its manufactures, the English traders made the best use of these concessions.

The small settlements were the first beginnings in the career of the foreign sea-merchants on the soil of India. The nature of their trade rendered it necessary for them to erect factories at these places for the purpose of storing up cargoes before-hand. Navigation to India was so expensive that "nothing was more detrimental" in the words of Orme "than long protractions of the voyage. Loss instead of profit would ensue, if ships were sent on the expectation of buying cargoes on their arrival. For either they would not find the cargoes provided and must wait for them at great expense, or if ready, would be obliged to buy them too dearly." The government of these settlements was in the hands of a joint stock company formed in England. To this company were given full powers of civil and criminal jurisdiction. To these, were gradually added powers of coining money and finally of making war and peace. Thus possessed of almost sovereign powers, the East India Company was a small state in itself, planted in a distant land.

Another note-worthy fact is that of all European nations, the English best understood the advantages of corporate life. The early development of a popular form of Government in England, had made English people quite familiar with the art of administration. The capacity for self-Government thus acquired carried the British flag into every quarter of the globe. By the close of the 17th century the directors of the Company had begun to entertain the idea of political ascendancy in India as a necessary adjunct of their commercial policy. "The increase of our revenue" they write to Fort St. George in December 1689 "is as much our care as the increase of commerce. It is that must maintain our force when twenty accidents might interrupt our trade. It is that must make us a nation in India. Without that we are a great number of interlopers, united by charters, fit only to trade where no-body thinks it their interest to prevent us."

Political Ambition.

Bengal was at the extreme limit of the Mogul Empire, and the hold of the Mogul Government on it was of the slightest. Its people were not a warlike race, and no great force was required and kept for its defence. The weakness of Bengal had not escaped the notice of the English, and they soon began to follow a policy of open aggrandizement. Under Shaista Kahn, the Mugal Government was on the alert. The power of Aurangzeb was at its height therefore a plan for the invasion of Bengal by the English ended in ruin and disaster. Aurangzeb pardoned them on intervention from Surat, after receiving a most humiliating apology, and restored their factories to them. The lesson of the war was not lost upon the English. They did not abandon their design, but busied themselves with secretly increasing their forces and strengthening their defensive works. And taking advantage of a disturbance, they obtained permission in 1699 to erect small forts round their factories for the purpose of defending themselves at the time of need. Moreover by offering a present to the Emperor's grandson Azimulshan, they obtained the villages of Chittantee, Calcutta, Govindpur as "Jageer." And when the Emperor was engaged in fighting the powersof theDeccan and subjugating the Marhattas,the English went on erecting works at Calcutta to which,in compliment to their Soverign,they gave the name of Fort-William. The disintegration of the Mughal Empire on the death of Aurangzeb gave them the opportunity for which they had been waiting so long. The provincial governors of the Empire had established themselves as independent Princes and set at naught the central authority.

A new scene opened in the Deccan. Here the French had established themselves and were pushing on their interests. The war that broke out between France and England in 1743 soon extended to India, and lasted till 1748. This struggle for the first time made apparent to the Princes of India, the existence of two rival European nations in India; and the vast superiority of their arms made these Princes anxious to seek their alliance in their own civil wars. Dupleix was at this time Governor of the French settlement of Pondicherry. The death of Nizam-ul-mulk, the Subedar of the Deccan, and the disputes that followed between various claimants to the throne, opened a field for the display of Dupleix's genius. The success of his policy forced the English to enter the lists against him. In the complicated succession contests, the French and the English fought as adherents of the rival Princes bnt in fact for their own supremacy. It was the daring and genius of Clive that finally secured the triumph of the English in Southern India.

The English had just succeeded in putting the French out of their way as rivals in the South, when Bengal became the scene af a fresh political crisis. On the death of Aliverdi-Khan, the Ruler of Bengal, the English of Calcutta, taking advantage of the youth and inexperience of his successor, began to strengthen their fortifications. When an cxplanation was demanded they treated theRulers messengers with indignity. Aliverdi,before his death,had told his successor of the apprehensions he entertained of the English. The young Nabob, Chirajudowla, therefore decided on inflicting a severe punishment on the insolent merchants. He seized their factory at Kasimbazar; and captured Calcutta. The news flew to Madras and brought Clive to the rescue. He retook Calcutta and made peace with the Nabob. Not the slightest trace of evidence is found in the records of the so-much made-of incident of the Black hole.

The Treachery.

Hastings, a young clerk, on being taken prisoner at Kasimbazar was brought to Murshidabad. Here his keen eye at once perceived that the administration of the Nabob was rotten to the core. Corruption and treachery were seen everywhere. He entered into secret plots for the deposition of the Nabob. The plots were discovered and Hastings had to flee for his life, The scheme remained in abeyance till again it was taken up and matured under the direction of Clive himself. When the plan was complete, Clive threw off the mask; and the so-called battle of Plassey transferred the real sovereignty of Bengal to the British. The gates leading to the territorial conquest of India were now thrown open before them. " Bengal " says Sir Alfred Lyall

" was the building site for the English Empire." Various views are held as to the nature of the English conquest of India. Sir John Seeley's view that the English conquest of India was made blindly cannot stand historical criticism; and has been ably controverted by Sir Alfred Lyall in his most thoughtful and admirable book "The Rise of the British power in India." But we have to bear in mind that the English conquest of India has no likeness to the Moghul conquest. The English rose to supreme power in Bengal by one of those revolutions which were so frequent in India during that period and which had enabled military adventurers to carve out principalities for themselves in different parts of the country. One such revolution had raised Aliverdi Khan to the sovereignty of Bengal. Another raised the English to that position. The English could not rest content with the acquisition of one province. They cast longing eyes on the rich plains that lay beyond it. The expansion of British Dominion followed as a natural result of the determination of the English to establish an Empire in India. Their progress was seriously imperilled at one time or another but in the long run, the superior diplomacy and skill of English statesmen won India for Ehgland; though the military force,—its superiority in arms and its wonderful discipline—also materially contributed to that end.

Battle of Plassey and the greed of Company's Servants.

It will not be out of place here to give an extract from the famous book 'Decisive battles of India' to show the significance of this battle. The battle, the consequences of which were so vast and permanent, was not of much importance from a military point of view, and it is not a battle of which any man or nation can be proud. It was only rank treachery that had driven the young Nawab from the field. Not one actor in that drama is free from the stain of dishonour. "To single out one," says Col Malleson "the chiefest of the conspirators was this Jaffer. To accomplish his personal end he hesitates not to become the perjurer of the deepest dye, to doom to a violent death the nephew to whom he had sworn obedience and to sacrifice the future of his country. If the people of India do indeed writhe under the sway of their foreign masters, they have to thank this Mir Jaffer Khan. This was the man who sold their three richest provinces to the English that he might enjoy the mere pageantry of royalty. It was indeed the merest pageantry. Soon was he made to learn that bitter truth, that by his own act, dominion in Bengal had departed from the Mogul. A tool, a cypher in the hands of the foreigners, for whom he had betrayed his master, he was allowed to govern, never to rule." It was not long before he grew tired of the yoke he had imposed upon himself, and he began to conspire with the Dutch at Chandora to shake it off. He was foiled in that attempt by the shrewdness and generalship of the English military and naval officers. Mir Jaffer was forgiven this time by Clive, but Clive left for England and was succeeded by Mr Holwell with other members of the Council who were most anxious to seize an opportunity of enriching themselves. They found Mir Kasim, the son-in-law of Mir Jaffer, a man who was wishing to buy them. A secret treaty was signed with him, by which Mir Kasim was to be placed on the throne of Bengal, after paying very large sums of money, as follows:—Mr Vansittart 5 lacs; Holwell 2 lacs, seven thousand; Sumner and Macguire each 250,000; Col. Caillaud 2 lacs; Col. Smith and Capt. Yorke 134,000; each.

The palace of Mir Jaffer was surrounded by the English troops; he surrendered himself and was sent to a private residence in Calcutta. Mir Kasim was a man of a different stamp. He wanted, from the very fiirst, to be his own master. He strengthened his position by removing his capital to Monger. He paid off all his obligations; he disciplined his army on the European model. The English were looking at these matters with suspicion, but the real cause of their breach with Mir Kasim was the excess of individual greed for money. Every servant of the Company wanted to enrich himself by having the monopoly of the trade. They wanted to buy and sell articles at their own prices, by which the whole province was falling into ruin. Mir Kasim, in order to put the Indian traders on equal footing, exempted all goods from duty. That incensed the members of the Council and they began hostilities against Mir Kasim. Patna was invaded and plundered. On hearing this Mir Kasim sent his army; the English force was defeated and made captive. Fresh English forces came up under Major Adams. Mir Kasim was defeated in the battle of Undhwanala and he fled to Nawab Shuja-ul-dowla. Shuja-ul-dowla, the Nawab Vizir of Oudh, accompanied by the Emperor Shah Alam, the second, brought an army to his relief. Again English generalship and European discipline was victorious at the famous battle of Baksar, which left the English, masters of the field. Mir Kasim fled away, Shuja-ul-dowla and Shah Alam threw themselves on the mercy of the English general. The English army was still at Allahabad when Clive again returned to India. He met the Emperor Shah Alam and received the grant of Diwani of Behar, Bengal and Orissa Northern Sarcars and the Jagir of Bussy.

Developments in the South.

While this was going on in Bengal many a development had taken place in the South. In 1753 the Marquis de Bussy, the French officer, by a sudden march on Aurangabad, had forced the Nizam to cede to him the districts on the north of Krishna River (Ganjam, Mauslipatam and Gantoon) which formed the Northern Sarcars. "These territories" says Orme "rendered the French masters of the greatest dominion both in extent and value that had ever been possessed in Hindustan by Europeans,not excepting the Portuguese at the height of their prosperity." This territory remained under the administration of Bussy till 1758. In that year a French Commander, Count Lally, arrived at Pondicherry with the express object of expelling the English from Southern India. He recalled Bussy from the command and appointed Conflans in his place. The departure of Bussy furnished a chance to the disaffected nobles to throw off the foreign yoke. Annandraz was their leader. He began to make overtures to the English in Madras and Bengal to get some military assistance. Clive, who understood the importance of Northern Sarcars, chose Lt. Col. Forde to command the expedition. Forde was one of those military officers who were instrumental in the building of the British Empire in the early days. The French officers who came to oppose the English in most cases proved to be made of very inferior stuff.

Conflans was no exception to them. He had so much of military and territorial strength that with half the courage and skill of Forde, he could have ruined him. Forde, simply by his daring and cool calculation, routed the French army in the battles of Kondor and Mausalipatam. He took Mausalipatam by storm and his feat remains unsurpassed in the history of India. By this victory he became master of the Northern Sarcars, which were soon formally ceded to him by the Nizam. That ended the chance of the French for power in South India. It was this territory which was formally granted to the English by the Emperor after the battle of Baksar.

Rise of Haiderali

In Southern India, about this time, Haider Ali was rising to great importance in Mysore. The Kingdom of Mysore was originally founded by a young noble who fled from the Court of Vijayanagar. Its first capital was at Hadra. In 1571 its Raja became independent of Vijayanagar and took possession of Srirangapatam, which he made his new capital. The dynasty gradually declined and the power passed into the hands of the family of ministers, a custom so well known in India. The minister Nangi Raj took part in the recent wars of Karnatic. In one of the sieges he was much assisted by a Mohammedan soldier named Haider. The father of Haider was a Naik. Haider had taken service as a peon and by good service rose to the command of two hundred. In the wars that followed he rose to great power. Nangi Raj placed him in charge of his fortress of Dindigul at the command of five hundred infantry. In the course of internal state quarrels he took the side of the puppet Raja and forced his benefactor Nangi Raj to retire and took all the power into his own hands. He then reduced to submission a number of independent chiefs, defeated the Marhattas under Murari Rao and nearly doubled the territory of Mysore, extending it up to the Coast of Malabar. In 1766 the puppet Raja died. Haider Ali took possession of the palace and become the supreme ruler in Mysore. Mohd Ali, whom the British had placed on the throne of Karnatik, became very jealous of the power to which Haider Ali had risen and he forced the English into an alliance with Nizam Ali of Deccan and the Marhattas to crush Haider Ali.

After a slight skirmish, the Nizam seceded from the war and made peace with Haider. Haider being hard pressed by the Marhattas offered terms to the English. The terms were rejected. Haider by a sudden march was at Madras and taught the English their mistake. The English were quite unprepared. He was master of the situation, and could dictate his terms, The English were compelled to make peace on the condition of mutual assistance during time of war. Haiderali was however soon at war with the Marhattas; the English evaded the fulfilment of the terms and refused to send him any help in spite of his repeated requests.

Rise of Marhattas.

Among the powers that had risen on the ruins of the Moghul Empire, the Marhatta State occupied the foremost rank. It was composed of a confederacy of four great chiefs among whom the conquered territories were divided; Scindhia and Holker had possessions in Malva or Hindustan. The Gaikwar ruled in Gujrat and Bhonsla in Berar.

The Peshwa, nominally the minister of the Marhatta Raja, the descendent of great Sevajee, was at the head of the confederacy. By this time, the Marhattas were masters of a great part of India. The Nizam and Haiderali paid them regular tributes in recognition of their Sovereignty. Their claims were acknowledged by the English in the Treaty they made with Haiderali. Alivardi Khan, Nabob of Bengal, had agreed to pay 'Chowth' (tribute) to the Raja of Berar. On the death of Aliverdi, the Marhattas were making preparations to conquer Bengal, when their attantion was drawn towards Upper India and the Afghan invader Ahmad Shah Abdali. For once they became masters of Delhi. Had it been possible for the Marhattas to conquer Bengal and to have secured the whole of Hindustan before the Battle of Plassey, Poona might have been the capital of United India, and the history of the country might have been quite different from what it has been. All the wars that resulted from the struggle for supremacy between the Marhattas and the English might have been avoided. The Marhattas had incurred the hostility of small states in their career of conquest and national consolidation. The advance of the English on the main-land was fatal for them. Fortunately for the English when Clive and his successors were engaged in establishing themselves in Bengal, the Marhattas assisted by other Hindu States, had to face a combination of Mohammedens under Ahmad Shah Abdali on the historic field of Panipat, where the former suffered a crushing defeat. The victor retired, and the fruits of the victory fell to the English. The next decade, during which the Marhatta Empire was recovering its lost strength, saw the firm establishment of the English power in India. During this period the English reduced the Nabob Vizir to a position of complete dependence on themselves; and made friendly alliances with the Nizam and Haiderali. Judging from their character, it was easy to foresee that they would make a bid for Empire. For this purpose they had retained the Emperor Shahalam as their pensioner in Allahabad. The possession of his person was to be a step towards the acquisition of that, for which his person was a symbol.

The bid for Empire

The Marhattas too under the able rule of the noble Madhorao had recovered from the disastrous effects of Panipat. Only ten years later, their armies under Scindhia and Holkar were again in the fields of Hindustan. With Delhi in their hands they were ready to take vengeance on Najib Rohilla who had been the principal cause of their ruin at Panipat. His country was over-run. Najib thus humbled readily submitted to them; their next objective was to secure the Emperor's person and take him out of the control of the English. The success of the plan at once brought them in conflict with the English. This point marks the beginning of the real struggle between the English and the Marthattas for the prize, which was no less than an Empire. The Emperor natuarally loved the throne of his ancestors. He left Allahbad in-spite of the protests and remonstrances of the English and re-entered Delhi in December 1771. He was forced to submit to conditions which ensured his dependence on the Marhattas, to whom he also made a grant of the districts of Allhabad and Corah which were his Jageers. The Marhattas soon threw aside all pretence of respect for him and prepared to attack the dominions of the Rohillas and the Nabob Vizir. Their power and the terror they had inspired were hardly less than before. They had again achieved that universal dominion over India which they openly declared to be their aim. "In the recognition of that fact and of the peril with which in common with other Indian Princes, our own provinces were threatened" says Sir John Strachy "lies the key to the policy of Hastings."

Warren Hastings.

Hastings had come a second time to India and in 1772 was placed at the head of the English administration of Bengal. He immediately formed his opinions on the position of affairs and on the relations of the English to Nabob Vizir, the Marhattas and the Rohillas. As to the Emperor and the Marhattas, he wrote in March that the powers of India laughed at the king's grants and that they were draining the country annually of 26 lacs for the purchase of a flimsy argument, intrinsically not worth 3 half-pence. "Yet for this idle pageant" he goes on, 'we have drained our country, which has a right to our protection, of its current specie which is its blood; and to this wrecthed King of shreds and patches are we almost to this day sending supplies of treasure, to enable the only enemies we have in India to prosecute their designs, which if successful must end in our destruction; because his home, authority, wealth and all he possesses, is theirs with his person." He had immediately on his arrival remonstrated with Mr Carter against "this man's being allowed any further payment." After some time, it was decided to stop the payment of the tribute to the Emperor and to the objections raised by Sir Robert Barker, Hastings replied as follows:- "The sword which gave us the dominion of Bengal, must be the instrument of its preservation and if (which God forbid) it shall ever cease to be ours, the next proprietor will derive his right from the same natural charter." The Calcutta Council assumed the government of Allahbad and Corah, but found it inadvisable to retain them on account of the distance from Bengal and the expenditure it entailed. The pretensions of the Nabob Vizir came next to the question of Emperor's allowance. His dominions were their natural barrier; he moreover offered great pecuniary advantage by agreeing to pay 40 lacs for the cession of the two districts to him. Shujahudowla's dependence on the Company had already rendered him unable to stand without the help of the English. "Among other curious instances" says Hastings "we proposed to him to keep a limited number of Sepahis. The consequence of this policy are such as were intended. He is now so weak that on every little alarm, our army must run to his assistance or he is in danger of being destroyed; and he is at the absolute disposal of the Commander-in-Chief." The success of this policy naturally gave rise to a system of subsidiary alliances, which was afterwards so effectively employed for reducing other states to the same condition of helplessness.

The Dispute Begins.

The Marhattas who were making rapid progress in their career of conquest, made preparations to take Corah and Allahabad. The news alarmed the Vizir and he turned to the English for help. The English had their own apprehensions on account of the Marhatta claims of Chowth on Bengal. Hastings immediately sent an army to assist the Vizir.

The Marhattas were so confident of success that they were considerably supprised at the refusal of Barker, the Commander of the English army, to concede their demands. Their military strength, however availed them nothing on account of the orders of recall from Poona. Suddenly they abandoned their pursuit and retired. The unexpected retreat was due to the changes that occurred in the Poona Government on the death of Madhorao in November 1772. "The root which invigorated the already scathed and extending tree" says the historian of the Marhattas; "was cut off from the stem; and the plains of Panipat were not more fatal to the Marhatta Empire than the early end of this excellent Prince."

The English were again free from the danger of Marhatta aggression.Theyspent the interval in consolidating their power. The Rohillas were a warlike race in the neighbourhood of the dominions of the Nabob Vizir. They might prove dangerous enemies to the English by becoming friendly to the Marhattas. To remove this constant source of weakness to the Nabob, Hastings determined to support him in his work of the extermination of the Rohilla race. The act was politic and conducive to the security of the English power. But to justify it on moral grounds, as is sometimes done, by contending that the Rohillas and the Marhattas were semi-barborous races, seems quite preposterous. The truth is that even the international morality of Europe in that period did not regard it a crime to exterminate a weak people for selfish aggrandisement.

Dissensions in Poona

While the English were thus increasing their power, their rivals were weakening themselves by internal dissensions. This period is the darkest in the history of the Marhatta Empire. On Madhorao's death, his brother Narain Rao,not yet out of his teens, succeeded him. On his death-bed, Madhorao had reccommended the young boy to the protection of his uncle, Raghunathrao. This man, the evil genius of the Marhattas, had only one aim, his own power, though it might involve the whole Empire in ruin. Before a year was out, a plot was formed to murder Narainrao. Raghunathrao and his wife had principal share in the crime. On the murder of Narainrao, the old Minister, Saccaram Bapu, who was indignant at the ascendency which his rival, Nana Fardnavis, a rising man, excercised over the young Peshwa, proclaimed Raghunathrao Peshwa. Nana fled from the capital for his safety. It was with great difficulty that he was prevailed upon to return on the assurances of forgiveness and restoration to favour. Raghunathrao distrusted the old ministers, but he did not feel himself strong enough to appoint others in their places. To make himself independent by having a devoted army at his back, he undertook in person an expedition against the Nizam. In the war that followed he suffered a defeat through the treachery of his own officers. In another action he recovered from the blow and made terms with the Nizam with the plan of preceeding towards Carnatic and enforcing his demands upon Haiderali. He was interrupted in this plan by the necessity of returning to safeguard his authority at home.

The distrust of Ragunathrao and his absence from the

capital, reconciled the ministers. On being found that the wife of Narainrao was with child, they joined in a conspiracy to deprive Raghunathrao of the benefit of the murder. Raghunathrao returned and inflictad a defeat on the army of the conspirators. But uhe birth of a son to the late Peshwa blasted all his hopes. The child was at once recognized as Peshwa by the ministers. Raghunathrao fled to Scindhia and Holkar, but finding them not well-disposed towards him, found refuge with the English at Surat.

English Intervention.

Madhorao had permitted an English resident to remain at his court. The resident, Mr. Mostyn who was noticing all these changes could not remain insensible to the advantages that might be secured. He encouraged Raghoba by every means to apply to the English for assistance. The Presidency of Bombay, who were on the look out for such an oppertunity, atonce concluded a treaty with Raghoba and prepared to restore him to the Peshwaship of Poona.

Such conduct, whose effects, the princes blinded by their self-interest could not fore-see, was the settled line of policy adopted by the Europeans in India, under the pretence of supporting the claims of one or the other claimant. Dupleix's genius had made this discovery. Under the pretence of spporting Mohemedali, the English established their influence in the Carnat i.c. Similarly under colour of putting Jaffir on the throne of Bengal, they gained mastery over the province. In the presidency of Bombay they had acquired no such influence. They longed for an opportunity which could give them some cause of interference; and when it came, they quickly grasped it.

Colonel Keating was appointed to the command of the army. At first he gained some slight advantages, but was defeated at the battle of Arras. All further operations were however stopped by the interference of the Council of Bengal.

Regulating Act of 1773.

By the Regulating Act of 1773 the President of the Council of Bengal was made the Governer General of all the English possessions in India, and the power of making war and peace was vested in the Council of Bengal alone. The presidency of Bombay, having not yet received the above information, had commenced the war. The Bengal Council considered this an infringement of their authority and resolved to annul all the proceedings of theBombay Council,by opening negotiations direct with the ministers of the Poona Durbar and ordered Col. Upton to proceed to Poona as their agent.

The Bombay Government, on receiving an intimation of the resolution, deputed Mr. Taylor, a member of their Council, to represent their case to the Superior Council. All his pleadings failed to induce the Council to change their determination. The Bombey Government urged the alliance with Raghoba in preference to that with the ministers. Their excuse for interference had more simplicity than reason in it. "Although" they say "we have not the plea of any injury sustained from the Poona Government, yet it should be noted that, that party was composed of the rebellious subjects of Raghoba." We should not however forget that the Bombay Government in taking that step were merely acting upon the commands of the Directors. The Directors had their eyes upon the districts of Salsette and Bassein, on the western side of India, though they would have preferred their cession by means of negotiations to taking them by war. By the treaty with Raghoba, the Bombay Government had secured for the Company, a territory with a revenue of nearly 250,000, per annum, apart from the territory ceded to the Company by Futteh Singh Gaikwar, the only Marhatta chief who supported the cause of Raghoba. To let slip such an opportunity would have been a neglect of the interests of their employers.

The Superior Council, too, on their part gave definite instructions to Colonel Upton to procure the cession of the two districts to the Company. Salsette and Bassein had been conquered from the Portuguese by Chimnajee Appa, the brother of Peshwa Bajirao. and added to the Marhatta Empire. The districts thus having been wrested by one of the Peshwa family,were regarded by the Peshwas as peculiarly their own property, and they ever manifested a jealous attention to the preservation of these acquisitions.

Col. Upton's Negotiations and Treaty of Purandhar.

The negotiations commenced early in 1776 on the arrival of colonel Upton at Poona. The letters which the Culcutta Council wrote to the ministers had fully persuaded them that Colonel Upton was deputed to treat with them on equal terms. "However" says the Colonel, "at a few meetings I made them sensible that they had understood these letters too literally." The ministers were determined not to part with Salsette or Bassein; and when Colonol Upton made the demand, they believed that he had exceeded his instructions. Colonel Upton explained the situation to his Council in the following words: "They ask me a thousand times why we make such professions of honour and disapprove of war entered into by the Bombay Government when we are so desirous of availing ourselves of the advantages of it. They say further that the Governor General and Council of Calcutta, have deputed me to negotiate, with them on terms honourable to both nations, yet all advantages and honour are confined to ourselves." They even refused the right of the Gaikwar to make any grant of teritory out of the dominions of the Empire.

Francis and his party were in majority in the Council. The Governer General, who at first was opposed to the war undertaken by the Bombay Government without the sanction of the Calcutta Council, changed his views and was inclind to support their measures. Francis, too, insisted on the cession of Salsette and Basein. Colonel Upton had instructions to give up Basein in the last extremity. On the 7th of March they received a letter from him saying that the treaty had been broken off. The Council finally came to the resolution of supporting Raghoba; General Clavering added the words "under necessity." The troops of the Company had not yet been withdrawn from him, and he was granting concession after concession to the Company. The Council prepared to write to both the Presidencies and all the chiefs, informing them of their resolution. But all these preparatory resolutions for war had to be revoked on the reciept of another letter on 1st April saying that the ministers had agreed to cede Salsette, and the articles of peace would be completed in three or four days.

The ministers at first offered a territory of three lacs instead of Salsette; but ultimately they gave their consent saying that they trusted entirely to the honour of the Gentlemen at

Calcutta who must be conscious of their having no right to these islands and would therefore restore them.

The ministers evidently gave way. It appears that they shrank from an actual contest with the English. It was not because they feared the English, but because they were divided among themselves. Raghoba had been once accepted asPeshwa and some of the ministers were still inclined towords him. The Gaikwar, a great member of the Confederacy, had openly taken his part. Scindhia and Holkar could not yet be fully trusted. Besides Salsette, the Company gained the district of Baroch, an adjoining territory worth 3 lacs.

The cessions made by Futteh Singh Gaikwar were to be annulled in case it should be proved that he had no power to part with them. The English on their part were to surrender Raghoba to the ministers. Such were the conditions of the Treaty of Purandhar which Colonel Upton concluded with the Poona Durbar. The execution of its terms lay in the hands of the Bombay Government. The Treaty could not be effective unless the Bombay Government agreed to it.

The Bombay Council Obdurate.

As the Bombay Government had no share in the conclusion of the treaty, they were determined not to carry it out. They protested against the loss of all the advantages gained by their treaty with Raghoba; and expressed their disapproval of the new treaty as injurious to the honour, reputation and interests of the Company. Mr. Taylor, who was at Calcutta finding his representations of no avail had already written to the Directors complaining of the interference of the Supreme Council. The Bombay Council informed Colonel Upton that Raghoba would not accept the terms stipulated for him and that they had offered him an asylum in one of their own settlements. Colonel Upton could only write to his Board so that they should direct the Bombay Government to comply with the conditions of the treaty; "Because" he said, "if Raghoba be permitted to seek a residence in the Company's settlements, the peace articles could not be carried into effect." Upon this the Board wrote in the strongest terms to the Bombay Government for compliance and made them answerable to the Directors and the Nation, if the Court of Poona should refuse to ratify the treaty and renew the war. The Bombay Government based their hopes on a fresh disturbance that occured in the Marhatta State on account of the rise of another claimant to the Regency in the person of Sadoba, who had escaped from prison. The Board however repeated their injunctions to them to conform to the conditions of the treaty and avoid any step that might expose them to the distrust and jealousy of the Marhatta State; and expressly told them to send Raghoba away, even by force.

The protractions and infringements of the Bomay Government considerably annoyed the ministers. They moreover had to undergo a heavy expenditure in maintaining the army which they could not disband as long as Raghoba was determined on hostilities. In their letters they complained of the countenance the Bombay Government has given to Sadoba's plans so bitterly as to approach the language of threats. They were afraid, they wrote, that they should be at last under the necessity of following the example of Haidar Ali who secured his peace with the English in a manner honourable to himself; that it was their resolution,if war again commenced,to carry fire and sword through all the Company's possessions, be the consequences ever so fatal to themselves. They allowed only a fortnight for the dismissal of Raghoba's forces. The defection of Raghoba's army immediately afterwards, however removed any occasion for the execution of the threat. Raghoba retired to Surat.

On the first of July 1776, the Board received the Director's letter declaring their intention of keeping all the territories ceded to the Company by the treaty of Surat. The Board considered such a course impossible and decided to adhere to the treaty of Purandhar,They forwarded the letter along with their own resolution to the presidency of Bombay. The effect of the letter on the Bombay Council was to strengthen them in their attitude of opposition. They at once signified to Colonel Upton their intention of retaining all the possesions without any regard for the treaty. In November they received Raghoba at Bombay, an act which caused great concern and surprise at Poona. The Governor General and the Council on the one hand demanded from the Bombay Council, an explanation of their conduct; and on the other instructed Colonel Upton to get leave of absence from the Poona Durbar, recomending an agent from Bombay for his place.

Such was the condition of the affairs when with much perplexity of mind Colonel Upton left Poona in the month of March and Mr. Mostyn again took his place in April 1777.

Difficulties of Hastings.

The domestic quarrels had thus weakened the Marhatta State and exposed it to the danger of foreign interference. When Nana was being baffled with these internal dissentions, the circumstances were not less critical for Hastings.

Since the close of the Rohilla war, the opposition in the Board had a majority. His authority was set at naught on every occasion. He felt so powerless that he had on certain occasions authorised his agent in England to present his resignation. Mr. Maclean produced the resignation in Nov. 1776. Two months before, Hastings had regained his authority in the Board on the death of Col. Monsoon, one of the opposition members. The resignation was accepted and General Clavering was appointed to exercise the powers till the arrival of a successor in Mr. Wheeler. The orders reached India in June 1777. Had Hastings been in the minority, he would haved retired without any struggle. Happily for England, he was then the master of the situation. He declared that he had never given positive instruction about his resignation. A strange scene followed: General Clavering held a Council with Francis; took possession of the records and sent for the keys of the Fort and the treasury. While Hastings along with Mr. Barwell occupied his chair in another apartment. An appeal to arms was imminent. Both parties however agreed to submit the dispute to the decision of the Supreme Court. The Supreme Court declared the resignation invalid. The arrival of Mr. Wheeler shortly after, would have deprived Hastings of all authority but for the death of General Clavering which left him again in the majority. He now proceeded to mature his plans for the consolidation of the British power in India. He cast his eyes on the map of India and beheld three detached dominions of the Marhattas, Haiderali and the Nizam each of them greatly superior in population to the large European kingdoms in the middle of the 18th century.

Haider was generally at war with the Marhattas. He had advised Raghunathrao not to trust the English " as they were deceitful people", assisted him with money and thus incurred the hostility of the ministers. The Nizam, outwardly friendly to the ministers, had sent an army to the help of the Peshwa ; though he watched every vicissitude of fortune, so as to turn it it to his own advantage. He made secret overtures through Fazal Beg Khan to Col. Upton for the restoration of Raghoba, provided he agreed to relinquish all claims to 'chowth and' make over Cuttock to the Company. Col. Upton rejected overtures but promised to keep them secret. At Delhi, on the sudden retirement of the Marhattas, the Minister Mujuff Khan had got hold of the Emperor's person and acquired complete control of affairs. He had enough work in dealing with the growing powers of the Sikhs of the Punjab. Of the members of the Marhatta Confederacy, Mudhojee Bhonsla, Raja of Berar, professed sincere friendship towards the English Company, though Nizamali expressed serious doubts of Mudhojee's sincerity.

Some changes had occurred in the Company's relations with the Nabab Vazir. The Raja of Benares died in 1773. On the earnest recommendation of the Bengal Council, his son Chet Singh's title was admitted and Shujahudowla confirmed him in his father's Jageer by the grant of a Sunnad. The object of the Council, as Mr. Barwell expressed it, was to bind the Raja by "the strongest tie of interest to support our Government in case of any future rupture with the Shujah of Oudh."

Shujahudowla died in 1774. He had not discharged

his debts to the Company. His only legitimate son, Mirza Aumany Asafudowla, who succeeded him, possessed neither the qualities of heart, nor of head. The Board at Calcutta decided to obtain the greatest benefits for the Company. They therefore held that their obligations, to the father, expired with him and in February 1775 despatched Mr. Bristew with fresh instructions to take the place of Mr. Middleton, the Resident at Lucknow. By the new treaty, concluded in the month of May, the sovereignty of Benares with a tribute of 22 lacs, was transferred to the Company. Corah and Allahabad were secured to the Nabab and the subsidy was increased to 2 lac and sixty thousand rupees per month. It is to be remarked that Francis and his party took great credit to themselves for having secured these advantages and no doubt gained the approval of the Directors. The Governor General on the contrary considered that extortion under such conditions was not honourable ; and asserted that the advantages could not be realised and were inconsistant with former treaties. The points of view too, uuderwent a change, when the positions of the parties were reversed.

THE POLICY.

"On the contrary, if it be true, that the British arms have suffered as severe a check in the Western World, it is the more incumbent on those who are charged with the interests of Great Britain in the East, to exert themselves for the retrieval of lhe nation's loss. That we have the means in our power; and that with such superior advantages as we possess over every power which can oppose us,we should not act merely on the defensive."—Hastings on Burgoyn's surrender in America.

Mr. Mostyn in the Poona Court.

A short time before Col. Upton left the Court of Poona, some Frenchmen had landed in Cheul and met with a cordial reception from the Durbar. Sakharam Bapu thought it proper to inform the Supreme Council of the harmless motives of the gentlemen who had come on behalf of the King of France to enter into friendly relations which the Government of the Peshwa. The Bombay Government were not slow in conveying their impressions of the visit to the Calcutta Council. They represented that the object of the visit was to have a factory at Poona and to obtain a port on the Malabar coast.

If the visit had any such object, it was quite harmless in the eyes of the Marhatta ministers, but the English could not view it in the same light. They apprehended serious consequences to their trade, and feared the operation of a dangerous influence in case of a war. The French were their rivals in trade. The English had experienced the effects of this rivalary in Southern India and wanted to be on their guard against a repetition of the story in the West. Further the Bombay Council had made up their mind not to keep the Treaty. They knew that war with the Marhattas was sure to come, and the presence of the French foreboded a serious danger to their plans. Mr. Mostyn, the former Resident at Poona, had taken his place again. He was well acquainted with the Court secrets and the party intrigues at Poona. The Ministers distrusted and suspected him as a fomenter of dissensions. On the appointment of Mr. Mostyn in place of Col. Upton, Nana at once concluded that peace was impossible.

The Bombay Government had instructed Mr. Mostyn to endeavour to excite the jealousy of the Marhattas, by representing the ambitious views and encroaching disposition of the French; and to make it his study to preserve the most amicable correspondence with the Durbar. The ministers saw through the weakness of the policy; and on their side, determined to play upon the fears of the French entertained by the English, just as the latter were intimidating the Marhattas by keeping Raghoba in their hand. Consequently the influence of St. Lubin grew more every day, and Mr. Mostyn was losing all influence at the Court. He was sometimes subjected to indignities of which he bitterly complained to his Government. The Bombay Government, thereupon, began to demand the dismissal of St. Lubin from

Poona. and then went so far as to ask for the payment of the expenses incurred by Raghoba at Bombay, which in the opinion of the Calcutta Council, was not only an infringement of the Treaty, but a voluntary aggravation of the offence.

In July 1777, Col. Upton had arrived back at Calcutta. His answer to the enquiries of the Supreme Board was clear and full. He told them that the Presidency of Bombay in every instance wilfully delayed and threw unwarrantable obstructions in the way of the conclusion of the treaty; and declared his firm opinion that the French intrigues would give no alarm when all the conditions of the treaty were carried out. Upon this, the Supreme Council wrote to Bombay, saying that there could be no reason to doubt that the presence of Raghoba at Bombay would continue to be an insuperable bar to the completion of the treaty; nor could any sincere cordiality and good understanding be established with the Marhattas as long as Raghoba appeared to receive encouragement and support from the English. He should therefore be positively required to quit the Company's dependencies and then added, "We shall hold you responsible for all the consequences of continuing the protection."

The Directors' Letters.

In the meantime. circumstances happened which strengthened the Bombay Council in their determination. In the first place, Mr. Mostyn succeeded in creating a strong faction emong the ministers against Nana. Nana was the only man who understood the critical condition of the Marhatta state. He hated Raghoba as a murderer; all the more because he had sought foreign intervention. He knew full well what the English aimed at by reinstating Raghoba in the Peshwaship. Sakharam, who was always jealous of Nana's growing influence and Moraba's party which could not see as far as Nana did, easily fell in with the intrigues oJ Mr. Mostyn. They all joined together to support the restoration of Raghoba under an English force. Secondly a letter was received in Bombay in December 1777, from the Court of Directors, in which they expressed their dissatisfaction with the treaty as it did not surrender Bassein and also with the mode of interference of the Supreme Council and lastly approved of an alliance with Raghoba if the terms of the treaty had not been strictly fulfilled on the part of the Marhattas. Thus encouraged, the Bombay Council wrote to Calcutta in plain words, that if Raghoba should not choose to accept the conditions offered to him, which, in their opnion, were certainly more spacious than solid, they could not bring themselves to remove him by force from their settlement. Then they explained to the Board the weak and divided state of the Marhatta Government and the feeble condition of its army which was hard pressed by Haidarali; informed them of their determination to anticipate the hostile machinations of the enemy by a prior attack, and in conclusion, pointing to the inadequacy of their resources, made an appeal for support.

We have seen how by a lucky chance the Governor-General had gained his power; and the future policy of the Supreme Council was to be his policy. On the former occassion he had not supported the measures of the Bombay Presidency. Now, besides having a knowledge of the sentiments of the Directors, he was informed of the divided condition of the Poona Ministry. He privately wrote to Mr. Hornby, the president of the Bombay Council, assuring him of his hearty support. In February 1778, he formally laid his proposals before the Board and said that the mutual infractions (real or supposed) of the treaty of Purandhar and the certainty of engagements entered into by the Marhatta Ministers and the French agent, made it incumbent on the English to be prepared for any emergency; therefore the Presidency of Bombay, "should be authorised to join in the plan to conduct Raghoba to Poona, to put forth the security of his person as a reason for their intervention; and to claim the port and the district of Bassein with territory adjoining Bombay or Bassein in exchange for Baroch, the prohibition of any European settlements on the coast of Marhatta dominions without the consent of the Governor-General and Council, and lastly the expenses incurred for the intervention." Finally he proposed that a military detachment be prepared in Bengal for the assistance of the Presidency.

The resolutions were carried and on 23rd March a letter was written to that effect to the Presidency of Bombay, but expressly stating that the sanction of the Supreme Council was given to the plan on the supposition that the cheif minister of the Marhatta State had particularly solicited their interference to settle the intestine quarrels of the state, and the object of their policy was nothing more than to promote the security of the Company's possessions by preventing the growth of an influence dangerous to the Company's interests and by defeating the intentions of a party adverse to the Company.

Changes in Poona Ministery

The condition however was not fulfilled. Sakharam and others refused to submit an application under their signatures. They soon succeeded in their object without the help of the English. By a sudden and quiet revolution Nana was driven out of the administration. When the new party, on coming to power, looked at the conditions of Raghoba's restoration, they perceived the wisdom of Nana's policy and declined to comply with them. "Should Nana condescend to make up matters with his opponents" so wrote Mr. Mostyn iu his letter of 29th March 1778, "it may induce the party not to comply wholly with Raghoba's treaty; and should Raghoba refuse to accept their invitation on any other terms, Moroba and his party might look upon themselves as absolved from the oath they gave to Raghoba"

So it happened. A few days after, in the first week of April a reconciliation took place. Nana was admitted into the administration. The attitude of Moroba towards St. Lubin remained unchanged and Mr. Mostyn found with much bitterness that his scheme had failed.

Col. Leslie's Detachment.

The detachment which had been ordered by the Board to assemble at Calpee under the command of Col. Leslie was now on its march towards Bombay by land. The march, known in England as a frantic military exploit of Hastings, was a subject of hot discussion in the Council. For several months the interest of the debates of the Calcutta Council centres round it. The opposition condemned the March as being full of difficulties on account of the approach of the rains, and the way lying through the territory of many country princes; and urged that a reinforcement whenever required could be easily despatched from Madras to Bombay. Their case was no doubt strong; and Mr. Francis missed no opportunity of repeating his efforts to stop the march and procure the recall of the detachment. The detachment, however, slowly marched on. It had to meet with a good deal of opposition and even open hostility when force had to be used. It had not been long on its way when Col. Leslie received an order from Bombay to discontinue the March. The Bombay Council had seen with great concern that the revolution had taken place in the Government of Poona without any application for their assistance. Their first impressions were hopeful. They had thought that the change would be followed by all the good consequences they had expected, including the destruction of the French influence. For the above reason and for some economic consideration, they judged it best to stop the advance of the detachment. In a few days they were disillusioned. Uncertainty prevailed in Poona and the dismissal of the French appeared as distant as ever. The new administration disappointed their expectation. Mr. Mostyn again wrote laying strees on the danger of the French intrigues. They immediately recalled the order they had sent to Col. Leslie and directed Mr. Mostyn to present a categorical demand to the Durbar in consonance with the directions of the Supreme Council as stated in their letter of the 23rd of March. He was required to ask whether the Marhatta Government was bound by the treaty of Purandhar; if so, whether they would immediately part with a territory worth three lacs as agreed upon in the treaty; whether they could give a satisfactory explanation of the presence of St. Lubin in spite of the frequent remonstrances made by Mr. Mostyn. A period of fourteen days was to be allowed, within which answers were to be given and any evasion on the part of the Durbar was to be treated as equivalent to a refusal.

Purandhar Treaty Broken.

The Governor-General's sanction of the plan of the Bombay Council had been given on the express condition that the chief minister in the State had solicited their assistance; and when they wrote to the Governor-General that Sakharam had refused to put his signature to the application, he in reply told them not "to become aggressors on any account but to continue to adhere to the strict letter of the treaty between the Company and the present administration of the Marhatta State." The President and Council of Bombay were so much impressed with this view that they wrote to the Directors saying "At last we may be obliged either to hazard the consepuences of acting without authority from them (Supreme Council) or passively behold the very existence of the Company endangered without making an effort to preserve it." In demanding the concessions from the Durbar, they fully understood that they were acting against the wishes of the Supreme Council, and openly recognized the fact when they said, "For we beg leave to observe that after the plan for restoring Raghoba had miscarried, it was impossible for us to defeat the designs of the French and not to break the treaty of Poona."

The paper of demands had been presented on June 4th. It remained unanswered for some time. In the meantime another revolution effected through Mahadajee Scindhia restored Nana to full power in the State. In answer to the demands of Mr. Mostyn Nana ascribed all delay to the English and expressed willingness on the part of the Durbar to come to a settlement. He said that the Sircar was sincere in desiring to keep the treaty, if the English kept it faithfully; that Futteh Singh had no right to part with the territory and a receipt of his letter to the effect, in the hands of Col. Upton was with the Sircar and that there was no agreement between St. Lubin and the Sircar (Govt.).

Mr. Mostyn refused all negotiations with Nana; closed with the other party and quitted Poona on the 13th July. It was on his evidence that the select committee of Bombay judged the answers sent by the Durbar to be unsatisfactory and considered themselves authorized to take measures to subvert the administration and establish Raghoba as Regent with the help of an English force. The Poona Durbar believed that Mr. Mostyn had taken advantage of the absence of Nana and had been guilty of many underhand practices. On his departure, Moroba and his party were seized and confined by Nana's orders. It seems an undoubted fact that Mr. Mostyn alone was the author of the line of policy pursued by the Bombay Government. He told them that Nana's Government was detested; that many principal officers would at once declare for Raghoba and even Scindhia would not oppose him; that Moroba's party could supply a force of thirty thousand men and the only course was to act conjointly with that party; and in conclusion declared "The sooner it is undertaken the better, for I cannot think there can be a more favourable crisis than the present." The decision of the select committee was based entirely on the judgment of one man who could not after all be infallible; and as the events showed, was wholly wrong. The monsoons were so uncommonly severe that the committee thought that they could not begin their operations sooner than the month of September. They communicated their resolution to the Supreme Council and expected to receive their answer by that time.

Col. Leslie had arrived at Chatterpore and was obliged to halt there for the repair of his artillery carriages. The Governor-General and Council had written to the Poona Durbar desiring free passage for the detachment through the Marhatta territory. The Governor-General further in his instructions to Col. Leslie required him to proceed to Bombay taking his route preferably through the province of Berar. On receiviug intelligence on 6th July that Mr. Mostyn had succeeded in obtaining a passport from Scindhia, and concluding that Col. Leslie might be tempted to prefer that route, he thought it necessary to issue positive injunctions to him to pursue his march through the province of Berar on account of the long and friendly intercourse which existed between the English Government and the Raja of Berar. Before the instructions were despatched, other intelligence arrived from Bombay that war had been declared between England and France. The Governor-General then issued peremptory orders to Col. Leslie "to march to Berar and not to pass beyond that province till further instructions from us, notwithstanding any order to the contrary from Bombay." Herein after all we get a clue to the policy of Hastings which lays before us the secret of the march of the detachment.

Hastings' own Plan.

Hastings had exposed himself to strong objections from the opposition on that question, but he had no mind to disclose his real design to them until it had been fully matured. He had however admitted on one occasion that the alliance with Raghoba was not the object of the measures which had been under taken by the BengalGovernment. Their declared object was to give security and permanence to the Government of the Bombay Presidency; and it was while they were pursuing that object that Raghoba was offered as an instrument and they accepted him as such.

The design of the Governor General was not a new scheme. It was a part of his main policy and was conceived so far back as 1773. At the time when he formed a snbsidiary alliance with the Nabab Vizir, he received an envoy from the Raja of Berar for an alliaece. Finding the envoy intelligent, he offered him tha same conditions, which, he said, were universally regarded as honourable and advantageons to both parties. On a domestic conflict between the two brothers each of whom claimed the throne of Berar, the scheme was dropped for a time. Hastings continued the intercourse and privately encouraged the envoy to keep the plan alive. Mudhajee the new Raja of Berar had been adopted by Sahu, the late Raja of Satara. Though on his death, the claims of Mudhajee had been defeated, he had a right to reassert them on a future occassion. The Raja of Satara sitting on the throne of the great Shivajee was nominally the head of the Marhata State. When the signs of troubles began to show there selves in Western India, Hastings had already resolved to take such preparatory measures as might secure his assis tance. An opportunity soon offered itself. In December 1777, Ram Raja (of Satara) died. As soon as the newly reached Calcutta, the envoy Beniram Pandit immediately wrote to Dewagur Pandit, the Dewan of Mudhajee advising him to persuade his master to assert his claims to the succession and to solicit assistance from Bengal. The Governor General himself wrote a similar letter to the Dewan in January, a fortnight before he received information of the plan formed at Bombay in favour of Raghoba. The military detachment ostensibly prepared for the assistance of the Bombay Presidency was in reality meant for Nagpor Hastings therefore insisted on its march by land. He kept his design a profound secret, resisted the daily importunities for its recall and waited, as he wrote afterwards, "for a clearer disclosure of the events on which its final determing tion should be concluded." But when the news arrived that war had actually been declared between France and England, there was no longer time to temporise: decided and speedy measures had to be taken.

The Governor General was convinced that the French has laid the foundation of an establishment in the heart of the Marhatta State and further that if St. Lubin could bring five hundred European soldiers and officers to discipline the nation army and get time to accomplish it, whatever party was in the posession of the Govt:, it would soon be in a condition to reunite the severed parts of that great Empire, to command peace and obedience at home, to apread terror over all Hindustan, and carry its ravages to the province of Oudh, and even attempt to dispute the possession of Bengal. "I resolved therefore" he concluded "to propose an immediate negotiation with Moodajee for an offensive and defensive alliance." "These," he himself has told us, "were not the reasons forcibly collected to defend a desultory measure, but the original motives on which it was projected and confirmed by the reflection of four years in which the subject had occupied my attention." In a long and well-reasoned minute, the Governor General drew the attention of the Board to the danger to which the British power was threatened by the machinations of the French. He argued that Bengal would be the distant object of their attack. Fort St. George possessed complete means of defence. Bombay was weak. The French had chosen the weak point for attack. They would work through Poona. "This is the abvious policy" said he "which the French must adopt if they seek to regain their influence in India; and it is no longer to be doubted that they have adopted it." "To guard against such a danger" he continued "ought to be our first object both for the immediate defence of Bombay and for the future security of Bengal." Then he dwelt on the necessitv of entering into an alliance with some great country power to counterbalance the suppossed confederacy between the French and the Marhattas. Moodhajee answered to the description. He was a natural enemy of the Peshwa. He would prove a most powerful and confidential ally with whom they should enter into the closest bonds of friendship. In order to accomlish it, they had to propose two advantageous inducements to him; the first was the support of his pretentions to the sovereign power in the Marhatta State; the second, the recovery of that part of his territory which had been seized by Nizamali; while on their part they would by such a connection possess a powerful barrier to their frontiers. He concluded by proposing that a servant of the Company should be sent to Nagpore for the purpose of negotiations.

Francis' Opposition.

Francis stigmatised the whole plan as a project in which distant shadows were pursued at the expense of solid and substantial interests and recommended a policy of moderation by asking the Bombay Presidency to make some concessions to the Poona Govt: "By pursuing even now a plan of maderation," said he, "with the Marhatta we shall propably take the most effective course for defeating the designs of the French and inducing the Mahrattas to relinquish any engagment they may have made with them." He had no objection to the treaty of alliance with Moodajee; but he was afraid of the proposed engagements, because he did not know whither such engagements might lead the Company's arms or how long they might implicate them in the political contests of the Country powers. All political connections in the rest of India were only important, so far as they affected them in Bengal. "Every accession of influence or possession elsewhere" he continued, "which by diverting our troops may prevent the exertion of our whole force, in case we should be attacked in this quarter, is hazarding a substance for a shadow." And lastly "I have no idea that if Moodajee Bhonsla has a ray of understanding and reflects on the fatal consequences which the Nabob of Oudh has experienced from his connections with the Govt: and which took their origin from a treaty of subsidy, he will ever suffer an English army to establish themselves in his country under any pretences whatever."

The truth is that the policy of Hastings was not as he professed, a policy of mere defence. Hs saw in the Marhatta State a danger to the English power, and he was determined to crush it. He assumed the necessity of defence to keep himself on the safe side. Neither did the opposition of Francis originate as is sometimes supposed, in malice. It was the result of honest difference of opinion on matters of vast importance. On one occasion Hastings put his case in the strongest language. "If Mr. Francis's positions" said he "were true that distant military expeditions were in themselves irreconcilable to the dictates of justice, honour and sound policy, great Britain ought not to be in possession of these provinces, nor of any other remote territory obtained by conquest. Had the politics of Great Britain been confined within such narrow limits as Mr. Francis would prescribe to those of this Govt: her power and opulence must have been unknown beyogd the seas which surround her." The reply of Francis was brief and simple. "The force of our army" he said "should be employed in securing what we have gained. All our acquisitions may be lost while we are endeavouring to extend them."

The Key-note.

Francis advocated a purely defensive policy. Hastings thought that it could not succeed as long as an aggressive power like the Marhattas was not checked in its career of aggrandisement. "I have held it" he said once "the best policy to meet the attempts of our enemies when we have just and reasonable grounds to expect them." For the time the policy of Francis seemed the right one. The policy of Hastings was more far-sighted and destined to bear fruit in the end. "No man in England or in India," he himself tells us," had studied the political state of India, and of its different powers with greater assiduity than myself; and no one had had better opportunities of knowing it." He saw with the fore-sight of a statesman that the dispute for supremacy in India, would lie between the English and the Marhattas. He knew further that the English could not engage with the Marhattas in an open struggle. He had recourse to the old plan of undermining the enemy by raising a puppet to power with the help of the British force. By a careful application of this plan he had twenty years before prepared the ground for Clive in Bengal. He himself wrote to Sir Eyre Coote as follows: "I had an early knowledge of Moodajee's pretentions and judged him, therefore a fit instrument to supply the place of Raghunathrao, in the plan offered to us by the Presidency of Bombay. He has wealth, power, and a territory extending from the borders of Bengal to Poona; Raghunathrao, neither wealth, power, nor territory, nor any influence which could supply the want of those requisites except what might eventually arise from an active part taken by the Presidency of Bombay in his favour; and they had plainly shown that they would take no more."

An objection wes raised afterwards to this method of Hastings by his enemies at home who condemned his statesmanship as an act of childish folly. It was said that if Mudhajee were raised to the dignity and power of RamRaja, the office of Peshwa would fall to pieces, and Marhattas being united under one head would again become formidable power. In a letter to one of his friends, Hastings replied to the above as follows: "The consequence which you apprehend, would not have happened. The same hand mhich had raised him to the sovereignty of the Marhatta State, would have been equally necessary to support him in the possession of it, and even of his existence. As a general position, I would venture to pronounce it as an infallible consequence that the English power in India will never, nor ever can be employed to raise one superior to itself; that in every instance, the reverse is most to be apprehended; that we commence as allies and end as tyrants and despots"

Here is the keynote to the policy of Hastings. If the policy did not succeed, it was due to circumstances which were beyond all human control. The sudden death of Mr. Elliot and the misconduct of Col, Leslie were the first blows to it. Its further operation was obstructed by the wild schemes of the Bombay Presidency. But above all there stood at the Head of the Marhatta State, a man who was a match for Hastings in all the qualities of a keen politician.

An Envoy to Mudhajee

The proposal of the Governor General was carried; and in July 1778, Mr. Elliot was sent as an envoy to the Raja of Berar with full powers to conclude a treaty of alliance. Instructions were despatched to Bombay and

Eort. St. George, advising the Presidencies, to communicate with Mr. Elliot about everything that might concern the negotiations, the object of which was explained to them. Moreover, orders were sent to Fort St. George to capture the French Settelments of Pondicherry and Mahe, Bengal itself having set the example by capturing Chandernagor. Such was the state of affairs when the resolution of the Bombay committee was received at Calcutta. This was the only occasion when Hastings showed a lack of decision. He wavered between two policies and did not see his way clearly. The sanction of the expedition to restore Raghoba meant the abandonment of his main policy. His envoy was to negotiate a plan with Mudhajee to enthrone him as the Raja of the Marhattas; and the Bombay Presidency required his sanction for an expedition to invest Raghoba with the anthority of the Peshwa: the one was incompatible with the other. There, no doubt existed a distinctiou between the office of the Raja and that of the Peshwa; and when pressed hard, Hastings had recource to that plea; but all real power was to rest in one person and the English could not with any consistency support the claims of two persons to the same authority. Francis was very strong on this point. He urged that keeping faith with the one, was a violation of it with the other. To escort Raghoba with a military force was not an advisable measure. It was highly probable that Mr. Elliot might have entered into engagements with Mudhajee totally incompatible with the instalment of Raghoba. He ended by saying "I think we should decide once for all which policy to adopt and what simple object we shall have in view. Our instruction then to Mr. Elliot, as well as to the other Presidencies may be formed on one determined plan. Otherwise I very much fear that each of the three Presidencies will act for itself and that for want of a concerted union of measures, no one of their respective plans will succeed.

The arguments were unanswerable. The Governor Genaral agreed with Francis; but thought it incumbent on him-self in that instance to support the measnres of that Presibency though against his 'befief of their taking effect,' Hastings did not follow a straight-forward course in swerving from the line of his policy; he committed a mistake of which he had to repent most grievously afterwards- He did something more. He acpuieseed though reluctantly in a measure which defeated the design which he had formed and which was so dear to him. The centre of policy was shifted and there arose a sort of coflict between the two different policies to be followed at two different places. This weakness on the part of Hastings iucensed Francis so much that he declared he would not take any further part in the business, as it was by means his view to embarrass measures when he could no promote their success.

The Conflict Of Plans.

On the first intimation of the failure of the project Mudhajee renounced all engagement with Hastinge. "That was" he tells us "the chief if not the sole cause of a sudden chauge in Mudhajee's disposition." On the disasterous result of the Bombay expedition he affirmed that he regarded the design as no less hostile to his Government than to Poona.

"I was strongly tempted" he says "at the time of drawing up Elliot's instructions to propose that an absolute restriction should be laid on the Presidency of Bombay, but my friend Mr. Barwell who was equally aware of the consequences of leaving them a latitude to defeat our measure, was of opinion that it could not be justified against the positive orders of the Court of Directors to renew negotiations with Raghunathrao in the event of a breach with the Marhatta Ministry, either convinced me or I wanted courage to take up so hazardous a responsibility against such an authority." The sanction of the Supreme Council was received at Bombay by the end of September. It contained the express provision that the engagements they were to form with Raghoba should not be contrary to those conluded with Mudhajee by Mr. Elliat, or of a hostile tendency to the Government of Berar. On the exact interpretation of this restriction there was much difference of opinion among the members of the committee. It was even thought that it might amount to a virtual prohibition. Some of them lamented the delay that had already occurred in carrying out their resolutions. Mr. Mostyn again strongly declared in favour of immediate action. On 12th October they resolved to carry out their plan into execution. end thus wrote to the Supreme Council: "If your letter was to be understood as containing a direction that we were absolutely not to undertake anything till we had heard from Mr. Elliot of the commission with the Bhonsla, it would have been equivalent to a prohibition of the expedition. we had meditated and which you had approved, by suspending it to so distant a period as to leave us little or no hope of success. We therefore thought ourselves warranted not only by your letter but by the most urgent plea of necessity to give our immediate and most strenuous assistance to Raghoba to secure the office of the Regent. The voice of people is with Raghoba and we are assured of a happy conclusion."

The Bombay committee had taken the fatal step. They appointed a committee of three men, Messrs Egerton, Mostyn and Carnac to lead the army; and then spent the whole of November in settling conditions with Raghoba. He agreed to the details after much difficulty. A manifesto was then drawn up in the name of Raghoba, addressed to all the Jagirdars, the Mutsadis and the people, and was freely distributed among the population. It contained an appeal to all classes to support the rightful cause of Raghoba and it further stated that the English had taken up arms to put an end to the disorders and give peace to the Marhatta Empire through him.

The Failure of the Expendition.

The expedition set out at the close of November. The enemy made no opposition till the 22nd December when they began cannonading from a distance. Contrary to all expectations none of the Marhatta chiefs ventured to join the standard of Raghoba. He told the committee in a message that he had been deceived. Mr. Mostyn was seized with a violent disorder and returned to Bombay where he died on the 1st of January. On the fifth of January Egerton resigned the command on the excuse of illness and even desired to proceed back to Bombay. The committee still decided to advance towards Poona, so that it might encourage the partisans of Raghoba to keep firm to their promises made to Mr. Mostyn. On the 9th, they arrived at Telegaon where they found a numerous army assembled to oppose them. The Marhattas had laid waste all the country and destroyed all means of supply. Their dissensions were forgotten under the necessity of uniting against a common enemy. The Government of Nana was not detested and Raghoba's name was not popular. The man who made assertions to the contrary and had raised false hopes in the Bombay Council was not alive to offer an explanation. Finding further advance impossible it was determined to fall back on Concan for supplies. The enemy got the intelligence and before daybreak the next day, made a vigorous attack which continued till the afternoon when the troops reached Wadgaon. The situation was very alarming, the commanding officer declared that they could not stand another onset and the committee found themselves obliged to sue for peace. The Marhattas demanded the surrender of Roghoba, the cession of all the acquisitions made by the English since the time of Madhorao and an order for the recall of the detachment. The committee plainly wrote in reply that they had no authority whatever to agree to such terms. The Ministers persisted and Scindhia asked the well known question "By what power then did you break the treaty made by Upton?" On 17th January the committee signed the paper containing the conditions and pledged their words for their due observance. Leaving Messrs Farmer and Stewart as hostages, the troops returned to Bombay. Thus were frustrated all the sanguine expectations of the Bombay Council, and such was the convention of Wadgaon, "an act so fatal to the interests of the Company and so disgraceful to the reputation and interests of the British nation" by which the English army submitted to the most humiliating terms.

The Court of Directors afterwards blamed the commanding officers for the slowness of the march which deterred the friends of Raghoba from joining his standard. This however does not appear to be the case. The fact is that Nana had restored perfect stability to the Government by removing the restless spirits who had given encouragement to Mr. Mostyn. Raghoba was cursed as a traitor and murderer. The Bombay Government had trusted Mr. Mostyn too much and reckoned without Nana and the general Marhatta feeling against Raghoba.

Deaths of Leslie and Elliot.

Where was the detachment when this calamity overtook the Bombay troops? Col. Leslie's progress had been very slow. By the 9th of September he had advanced only 120 miles and had incurred an enormous expense. In direct opposition to the orders of the Board he began to meddle with the domestic affairs of the Princes of Bundelkhand. Even the news of the war between France and England and the consequent urging of the Bombay Presidency produced no effect on him. The Board finally decided to dismiss him from the command and appoint his second Col. Goddard in his place, Col. Leslie was saved by death from disgrace. His successor possessed all the virtues that he lacked. Col. Goddard at once made up all quarrels and resumed his march. All obstacles that had frightened Col. Leslie vanished before his determination. He combined in himself the qualities of an effecient military command with those of a discreet politician. "We all admire Col. Goodard" Hastings once said about him, "his conduct is distinguished by a spirit of enterprize and activity. I cannot detect any error committed by him or any advantage neglected by him."

Hastings' hopes of a fruitful alliance with Mudhajee received a great shock by the sudden death of Mr. Elliot on 13th September. When the news reached Calcutta, the opposition again urged the recall of the detachment and advocated the sound policy of leaving the Marhattas to settle their own affairs. to endeavour to cure rather than to foment their jealously. The Governor-General was nevertheless sanguine of the success of the negotiations. He laid much stress on the enormous strength of Mudhajee and his hostillity to Poona, which the armies of Berar had once reduced to ashes. He was hopeful of the execution of any design made in conjunction with Mudhajee and finished by complaining of the uncandid advantage that was taken of the misfortune into which he was thrown. In November, Col. Goddard was invested with the powers formerly given to Mr. Elliot. Col. Goddard received no communication from the Bombay Council about their resolutions. At the time when the Bombay expedition was proceeding towards its fatal end, he was carrying on negotiations with Mudhajee. Mudbajee had offered him a warm welcome. He sent one of his courtiers, Jadorao, to receive Goddard at the Nurbudda. Col. Goddard found Jadorao most friendly to the English; but he was not empowered to talk on the subject of an alliance. Col. Goddard lost no time and sent Lt. Weatherstone to

Nagpur. The Lieutnent noticed a great change in Mudhajee's attitude. He was told that the five months delay of Col. Leslie had been very impolitic and prejudicial to their designs. The news had spread far and wide. The Poona Government had set about raising and discipling their forces. All the chiefs were on their guard. Nizamali was in close alliance with the Peshwa's Government. Mudhajee therefore wanted time and offered to send a person to Calcutta to make some final settlement. Another objection that he raised related to the part taken by the Council of Bombay in favour of Raghoba; "The Court of Nagpur had addressed your Government" thus wrote Goddard "and have solicited as well as recommended the relinquishing of the cause of the latter and accepting the terms from the Ministerial party; and the motive, they acknowledge, for acting this mediating part, is to pave the way for the advancement of their schemes hereafter, which they profess cannot be done consistent with an attitude to the interests of Raghunathrao This has destroyed all hopes of concluding an alliance with Mudhajee."

In answer to the appeals of Hastings to Mudhajee that he should not miss the opportunity, and himself guide the operations of the detachment along with his own army, he gave a straight-forward answer. "It is not to be done at once" wrote Mudhajee, "but requires time to regulate matters of such importance. The junction of a small body of my forces with yours can produce no good effect, but remove the veil from the business, and have our designs exposed;

and still more it will expose my dominions to the ravages of the armies of the Peshwa aud the Nizam."

In the midst of these negotiations Col. Goddard received a letter from Bombay which informed him that the expedition had started. He broke off the negotiations, and on 6th December left for Surat. The next information he received, was from the letter, written under one of the stipulations of the convention directing him to march back with his army. Three days after however, he received another letter telling him to pay no regard to the previous letter and the orders contaiued therein.

Goddard hurried his march; escaped the Marhatta army, sent to harass him; and by the end of February reached Surat,

Arrangement With Scindhia.

On the return of the army to Bombay, the President at once declared that the convention was not valid, and despatched Mr. Hornby to Calcutta to supply the Governor Geueral with all the information and details of local knowledge that they might require, or that might be necessary for the success of their plans. Before the instructions could arrive from Calcutta he proposed to exert himself to extricate their affairs from the entaglements with which they were beset. To the partialitv of Scindhia they were indebted for the more favourable terms of the convention. It was due to him that the point of detaining the whoie army as hostages which Nana required, was given up ; and by that means they had it in their power to disavow the convention. Mr. Hornby now proposed to make an attempt to alienate Scindhia from Nana and engage him in the English interest by investing him with the headship of the Marhatta Empire which was his proper right. In his opinion the alliance with Scindhia was even preferable to the favourite project of the Governor-General.

The Governor-General approved of the plan. He realised the importance of the high position held by Scindhia and appreciated his best service by remarking that "his was an act of kindness that a nation could have received from the bounty of an individual." Sir Eyre Coote expressed the view in clearer terms. "Our real interests are" he said, "to keep theirs divided, always preventing overgrowth of power in any of the parties, thus endeavouring to hold the scales in our hands, we remain ourselves a great degree the umpire. This is the truest road to the support of our dignity and profit as well as the surest means retaining undisturbed what we now possess. I therefore think that at present we should not seek to renew a war, But if by refusing this, they force us to continue hostilities, I must in that case suppose a junction of all their parties and of course, a union of all their forces."

Col. Goddard in marching towards Surat had acted on his own judgment, as he knew that his action was consistent with the spirit of his instructions. The Governor-General and Council were so pleased with this prompt action to save the Bombay Presidency from utter ruin that they appointed him to the independent charge of the expedition. On receiving the orders, he announced to the Poona Durbar on 5th April that he was empowered by the Supreme Council to conclude a seoarate alliance with him.

The Governor-General thus summed up the whole situation and declared his future policy: "The greater loss which we have suffered by the late disaster, is in the discredit which it has reflected on our military reputation. We should take care not to betray our consciousness of weakness and distrust in our measures. At all events while we seek for peace we ought at least to be prepared for war as the surest means whether immediate or remote to obtain it."

THE GREAT COALITION.

"The English nation is a thorn in our side, which is to be got rid of". "I am not inattentive thereunto," replied Nana *"and shall leave no means untried for that purpose."*

Hastings' Apologia

The expedition had failed. Its consequences were more far reaching than the Presidency of Bombay or of Bengal had ever imagined. The Governor-Genral learnt of the disaster in February 1779. In his opinion, it was a terrible blow to the prestige of the English. He determined not to ratify a tittle of the treaty or convention of Wadgaon, and to risk everything for the re-establishment of British credit in India.

The expedition was not his act. He had no part in it. It was rather undertaken against his wish, and it spoiled his designs. "The Marhatta war" he said afterwards in surprise "has been and is yet called mine. God knows why; I was forced into it. I professed no other design but to support the Presidency. The precipitate expedition to Poona and the infamous surrender were events beyond the reach of human fore-sight. Perhaps when I shall cease to be an object of persecution, the preservation of Bombay may be ascribed to me. My part was no more than a salutory interposition of extraordinary means of the correction of effects derived from the blunders of others." Henceforth the whole affair became his concern. It was his policy that guided every movement on all sides. He had to adopt the policy under circumstances which were not of his creation, it was none the less his policy and he was to be held responsible for its consequences. On receiving authentic information from Bombay, he invested Col. Goddard with full powers as the minister of the Bengal Government to treat with the Peshwa and Ministers for the renewal or confirmation of the treaty of Purandhar.

He laid down the provisions that the Ministers should recede from all the pretensions acquired by their engagement with Messrs. Carnac and Egertono, and engage never to admit any French force into their dominions, nor allow the French to from any settlement on the Marhatta coast. The rejection of these terms was to be made the basis of war.

To the Poona Durbar, this threat conveyed the loss of all the advantages they had gained from their signal success over the English army, What was a mere mishap in the eyes of Hastings, was looked upon by Nana as the fruit of his persistent and comprehensive policy.

Activities of Nana.

To form an estimate of Nana's activity, we should bear in mind that if Hastings suffered from the disadvantage of being served by inefficient men. who could not carry his plans into action, Nana laboured under the same difficulty in a still greater degree. The Peshwa was young. Nana was one of the Ministers of the Peshwa. The rest of the chiefs acted upon his advice only so far as they could grasp it, or as it suited their own purpose. At the time, Moroba was plotting with Mr. Mostyn to bring about the restoration of Raghoba, Nana had to satisfy Scindhia and Holkar by offering them bribes in order to secure their adhesion to his party. On the re-appointment of Mr. Mostyn, he clearly saw that the English had no wish to observe the treaty. He distrusted Mr. Mostyn as the fomentor of dissensions; and laid restrictions on his communications by placing spies in every direction. Even the by-roads were not free, and rarely a letter could pass without his knowledge. By treating Mr. Mostyn with scant courtesy he wanted to bring home to him the fact that his presence was not welcome in Poona. On one occasion he was openly told to leave the town. Mr. Mostyn suffered all the indignities and stayed. He knew that his departure from Poona was against the interests of his employers. He kept the Presidency informed of the movements of Nana, the object of St. Lubin, and all important secrets connected with them, which he obtained through the agent of a Raja who kept Nana's munshi (Persian writer) in his pay.

In May 1778, Nana wrote to the Nizam as follows:— "Now a disturbance has taken place on account of some persons who do not understand justice. They have sent for Dada (Raghoba) to Bombay. But you make yourself very easy that they can do nothing. Sakharam has joined me heartily. I hope that you will on my calling send Jaffir-udowla Bahadur with an army this way directly and you will also come and abide at Aurangabad in order that through fear of you, nobody may raise up his head. Through the hands of the English nothing will be done because I have made a treaty with the French by means of their Vakeel, for the punishment of a nation who have raised up an insolent head and whose measure of injustice is now full." The Nizam was avowedly attached to the Poona Ministers. He remonstrated with the Supreme Government against their designs in favour of Raghoba and pointed out that on account of the treaties, a moral obligation rested on him to help the Ministers.

Nana, then wrote a similar letter to M. Bellacombe, the Governor of Pondicherry, saying that the English were faithless and quarrelsome and fomented disturbances, the principal actor in which was Mostyn, the Vakeel of the settlement of Bombay, who laid the foundation of our quarrel with English. He further offered the Governor 20 lacs of Rupees and 10 ships of sepoys in case he consented to make an attack on Bombay. This letter reached Bellacombe when he was engaged in repelling the English in the seige of Pondicherry. He promised to start for Bombay as soon as he had done with them. But his real feelings are expressed in his letter to St. Lubin, in which he says, "In the present situation of French aflairs, we are not in a position to consider of great enterprizes. The best way was to remain quiet. The steps, the English were following, would sufficiently disgust the different states in Hindustan, and the French then might at a more convenient juncture stand forth to advantage. We have nothing to do at present but to start the game for the English to pursue." That such was the general line of policy marked out by the French, becomes evident from a note that was fonnd in the papers of M. Chevallier which were seized by Mr. Elliot in July 1778. "It would be proper for me" it ran "to apprize the Marhattas at Cuttack and Berar of the disposition of the English respecting a war wich appears to be inevitable; that I should write to those at Poona that this is a moment to unite inorder to crush that ambitious nation who hath already met with considerable losses in America which they seek to repair by subjecting all the Princes af India." St. Lubin himself thus acknowledged in his letter to the Portguese Captain General of Goa that his mission was secret and so stripped of all honours; that his stay there was not agreeable to the English as they were doing everything in their power to have him dismissed; and that he had notwithstanding been able to carry out his designs.

Then Nana turned to Moodajee, and tried his utmost to dissuade him from joining the English. Moodajee in proof of his friendly desire had got M. Chevallier arrested in Cuttack and delivered over to Mr. Elliot. His impatience for the alliance was so great that on the death of Mr; Elliot he expressed a strong wish that the sad event would not prove the means of discontinuing the negotiations for an alliance, "the fame of which had gone forth and alarmed the fears of the Peshwa and the Nizam." We have seen how the importunities of Nana, added to the part taken by the bombay Council in favour of Raghoba, had almost reduced him to despair. He asked Col: Goddard what replies he should make to the enquiries of the Poona Durbar; and even persuaded him not to run the risk of advancing in the face of large armies. The Governor-General had for a time relinquished all thought of concluding a treaty with him though "still retaining a lasting rememberance of his kindness."

Moodajee's Hesitation.

The disaster to the Bombay troops that followed. made a deep impression on Moodajee and convinced him of the wisdom of the course he had adopted. Upon this, he wrote to the Governor-General "You write me that there was no necessity to have written voluminously and that one line was sufficient to have given an answer to the proposed designs that is to say, "Your forces are arrived at Hoshangabad; my troops shall join them and should settle the business." This causes me real surprise. The end of it would have proved a parallel to that of the English at Bombay. To oppose a mountain, a mountain is requisite; what effect would be produced by throwing pebbles at it. By the blessing of God, you are known to have great experience in business. Regard what I have written above as dictated solely by warm friendship and on considering maturely you will approve thereof." Finally he recommended a settlement with the Marhattas and offered to act as mediator himself.

At the desire of the Durbar, Moodajee had already sent his Dewan Dewagur Pundit to Poona. Nana's object was to force the court of Nagpore to join a general Coalition against the English. Now that the expedition had ended in disaster, and the repudiation of the convention by the English had rendered them guilty of an open breach of faith, the disposition of the Ministers and the intensity of their resentment may easily be concieved. They could never rest satisfied with the advantage they had acquired over those who had matured such dangerous designs against them. "Thus" said a Madras letter "by one ill-timed and unfortunate enterprize, the reputation of our arms is sullied and the friendship of the principal states hazarded or lost for ever; and that too at a time when we are engaged in a war which calls for the exertions of all our forces and the good-will of every State in India."

The progress of coalition.

Nana at once set to work and exerted every nerve and fibre to bring about a coalition of all the other powers of India for the extermination of a race which had no regard for treaties. His emissaries were in the imperial Court to induce Nujuff Khan to become a party to it. He carried on negotiations with the French and the Portuguese settlements. He offered advantages to the Dutch at Surat if they could supply him with arms and ammunition. His agents opened negotiations with the Nizam and Haider. In the meantime an unexpected development in the South brought both the Nizam and Haider closer to Nana.

When the news of the declaration of war between France and England reached India, the Supreme Council had ordered the Presidency of Fort St. George to capture the French settlements of Pondicherry and Mahe. The latter was on the coast of Haider's dominions. Haider's relations with the English were far from being friendly. The English had evaded the fulfilment of the treaty concluded with him in 1768 when Haider was engaged in a war with the Marhattas. In 1778 being again at war with the Marhattas he had renewed his offers of alliance to the English on the basis of mutual assistance. "Indeed" wrote the President of Fort St. George "The treaty concluded with him in 1769 appears to us fully to express the conditions on which we may now secure his friendship and if that treaty had not been evaded by the former Government here, we do not believe that Haider would desire any new engagments at this time or that it would be necessary for us to conclude any with him." On the surrender of Pondicherry to the English in October, Haider made a show of formality by writing a congratulatory letter to the Government of Madras. But he strongly protested against their designs upon Mahe which he considered under his protection. The success of the English had kept him neutral. They might have pursued their operations to the point at which they aimed, without any molestation from him, had not the misfortune of the Bombay troops caused a material change in the situation of affairs. At the moment the news of defeat arrived from Poona, the question arose as to whether it was safe to go on with the expedition which had been set on foot. There was risk and inconvenience in sending troops out of the Carnatic, but the plan if successful was calculated to bring great advantages. It would wipe out the unfavourable impression, produced by the late defeat, while any appearance of timidity or diffidence would confirm them and would probably be more prejudicial to the interests of the English than any failure that could result from the prosecution of the enterprize; and lastly the withdrawal of troops would be inevitably followed by the capture of Tellicherry by the French, which, though perhaps not important in itself, would be considered a victory of no small consequence to the French. These considerations drove the Madras Govt: to the conclusion that the expedition should be undertaken. The command was given to Col: Braithwait Mahe surrendered on February 19th. Haider had told the English that if anyone entertained designs against those traders whom he considered his subjects, he would no doubt adopt the best and most considerate method of giving them assistance. It was better to keep peace he said; and the words were not uttered as a mere threat. Haider at once took Cuddapah and was making preparations to invade Guntoor when he was interrupted by the approach of the Marhatta army on the other side. He quitted his conquests and marched back to Seringapatam leaving a part of his troops in the Cuddapah territory.

The question of the Circars.

The English were bound to defend the Guntoor Circar which, a short time before had been taken by them under their protection. By the treaty concluded with the Nizam in 1768. the three Northern Circars were made over to the English on payment of a fixed annual Peshcush (tribute). Guntoor, the fourth Circar, was given to Basalat Jang brother of Nizamali, with reversion to the Company. The Circars were the Jageer of Bussy. It is no wonder then that a remnant of the French army, about 500 troops, had entered into the service of Baslat Jang. This circumstance came to the notice of the Madras Government in 1775. They drew the attention of the Supreme council to it and obtained full authority from the council to procure the dismissal of the French troops by negotiation or otherwise.

But they contented themselves with opening a correspondence with the Nizam on the subject which came to nothing. When the French alarm again became formidable, the presence of these troops in the neighbourhood naturally excited the fears of the Madras Government. The danger was increased by the fact that the port of Mootapilli in the Circar of Guntoor supplied the opening by means of which, the French could easily land troops and stores on that part of the coast. It is to the credit of the Madras Government that they had recourse to the easiest expedient in getting rid of the danger. It is incorrect to state, as is sometimes said to have been the case, that Basalat Jang, alarmed at the hostile designs of Haider and anxious to secure the assistance of the English agreed to rent the Circar to the Company. It was on account of the persistent supplications of the President Rumbold that the Nabob of the Carnatic, the old ally of the English, prevailed upon Basalat Jang not only to dismiss the French troops, but to make over the defence of the Circar to the English. He consented to make himself this offer to the Presidency of Fort St. George. In November 1778, his Vakeel signified his master's desire of renting the Circar to the Company. The articles of the treaty were properly drawn up ; and it was thought right to make a fresh application and request the Supreme Council to favour them with their opinion as to the provisions of the treaty ; and forward their sanction if they approved of it. The whole question then with a reference to their sanction given in 1775 was again referred to the Supreme Council.

The treaty with Basalat Jang was afterwards made a subject of much discussion. Hastings disclaimed all con nection with it. It is held, by a very high authority that the treaty never received the sanction of the Governor-General. The words therefore which occur in the reply of the Supreme Council dated 25th January 1779, are worthy of note in this connection.

"In regard to the alliance proposed to be formed with Basalat Jung" they say "we highly approve of the measure in general and leave it to you to negotiate and finally conclude a treaty with him." The alliance was conformable to the policy of Hastings. He added his own recommendations to each of the articles which he carefully went through. He suggested that the subsidy should be fixed at the largest amount that would probably be expended and that troops to be maintained for the service of that chief should be as far as possible restricted to the natives, in order that the European force might not be weakened by the alliance.

Haider had attempted an invasion of Guntoor. On 2nd April Basalat-jung made an application for the stipulated troops on the grounds of the invasion he feared. The Presidency of Fort St. George took this occasion to return the threat to Haider. While professing to base their claims on his friendship they asked him to desist from any attempts on Basalat's territory as the Company was pledged to defend him and by the blessing of God powerful enough to avenge any injury offered. "Once provoked into hostilities" he was thus warned, "they will not fail to exert all their strength in punishing the offender and with justice on their side, they have no doubt of success."

They resolved immediately to send 3 battalions, a company of artiallery and six field pieces under Col: Harper for the protection of the country of Basalat Jang. At the same time, they were conscious of their distressed condition and entreated the Supreme Council to unite all the forces of the three Presidencies to crush the dangerous enemy by a joint attack on his two principle cities, Mangallore and Seringapatam.

Mr. Holland at the court of the Nizam.

There was yet another thing. The sovereignty of the Circars belonged to the Nizam. Basalat Jang was his dependent. The English had made a treaty with Basalat Jang without obtaining the Nizam's sanction or approval. Moreover they had not paid him the usual tribute for the other Circars for several years. Having taken up such an hostile attitude towards Haider, they were naturally anxious to be acquainted with the Nizam's feelings towards them. So as to evince a desire to establish a closer connection with him, they appointed one of the Company's servants, as their resident at his Court. Mr. Holland reached Hyderabad on 6th May. He was received with great honour. He found the Nizam jealous of the growing power of Haider and favourably disposed to an alliance with the English against him. The information of the friendly treatment shown to Mr. Holland encouraged the Presidency in their hopes and they now began to look forward to the total remission of the Peshcush. Only a week after, the negotiations underwent a complete change. Mr. Holland received advices from Madras saying that a force had been despatched for the defence of Basalat Jang's territory against Haider. The Nizam was startled at the news. He told Mr. Holland that affairs of this nature were attended with serious consequences and required mature deliberation. He further declared that the correspondence and the alliance with his brother, was a direct infraction of the treaty of 1768. He insisted on the necessity of forbiddig the sepoys from advancing into his country or else, he said, he would be obliged to order his forces to oppose their march. A month later, before the Council of Madras had been informed of the change in the Nizam's attitude, Mr. Holland received further instructions to the effect that he should represent to the Nizam that the Peshcush was a very heavy burden and to endeavour to obtain remission or reduction of it. He was specially asked to achieve this end by appealing to the friendly disposition of the Nizam.

No sooner had Mr. Holland opened the subject, than the Nizam burst into a fit of anger and said he knew that the English were determined to violate the treaty. "His excitement" wrote Holland "was very great, and he spoke as if Haider was waiting only to be called on to join him. His language was of resentment and war."

Yes, that was true. The Nizam had just received a letter from Haider protesting against the step taken by Basalat Jang as a measure incompatible with prudence and foresight. "In every part throughout Hindustan" said Haider "where the English have established their influence and got a footing under the cover of giving their protection and assistance, experience has shown what treatment those have met with, who have had any connection with that nation. It may be seen by their conduct towards the Nazims of Bengal and Oudh, whom they have stripped of everything and reduced under their authority. His Excellency no doubt did not attend to all these considerations, when he thought of entering into an alliance with them: for if he had, it is probable he would not have consented to it. It is my opinion that the English should not be allowed to have a footing in that part of the country." Then he pointed out that all difficulties could be settled by renting the Circar to his Killadars. Nobody would dare attack the country if such an alliance was made with him. It was not in his power to consent to His Excellency's giving up the Circar of Guntoor which adjoined his country, to his old and bitter enemies. "What are the English" he concluded "whose name gives so much alarm to the people of this country. How did I encounter them when I was at war with them. How often were they not defeated by my victorious troops. This is well-known to everybody. Why should they be so much feared that their protection should be solicited." Such offers of friendship put an end to the Nizam's jealousy of Haider and his determination was now fixed for a time.

The Nizam immediately wrote a letter to Basalat Jang in which he repeated all that Haider had communicated to him and recommended that the Circar should be rented to Haider, because "we shall be able to recover when our power increases, any country he now takes from us. But it is highly improper to throw so much power into the hands of Europeans. You have done wrong in following this step." Then the Nizam asked him about his future intentions and concluded with the threat, "If you persist in doing this, you will suffer the evil consequences of it."

Instead of acting up to the advice given to him, Basalat Jang showed great impatience to have the detachment with him. In May a deachment under Col. Harper had been sent to Mootapilli and thence to march to Adoni to his help. The march lay through Cuddapah, which had lately been conquered by Haider. A large body of Haider's men guarded the passes and opposed the march of the English troops. Col. Harper had to fall back on Iccocanda and was usable to renew his march for want of money and provisions.

In Augnst, on the one hand, the Council of Madras wrote a long letter to Haider, in which they complained of the opposition offered to the passage of their troops and observed that it was the invariable practice of all powers in a state of friendship to let their troops pass and repass through their territories. They were however willing to persuade themselves that his manager acted on the occasion without his knowledge or authority. On the other hand, they were much displeased with the delay caused by Col : Harper and appointed Col, Baillie to command in his place. Col, Harper had in the meantime set out on his march and was stopped in his advance by Basalat Jang.

The Nizam and Haiderali

The Nizam wrote to Haider that he was prepared to join him to prevent the English from entering his territories. Haider at once took possession of Basalat's country, confined him in his palace, and threatened to destroy him and his family, if he did not discontinue his correspondence with the English. The Nizam then being apprised of Basalat's situation wrote to him again, that if he would renounce all connection with English, and regain possession of Guntoor, he would be restored the territory that had been seized by Haider, and if the English did not immediately march out of tbe country, the territory would be bestowed on Haider and he himself would join Haider for the expulsion of the English from the Carnatic.

Under these circumstances, Basalat Jang was obliged to submit. In November the detachment returned again to Icconanda. The Select Committee of Madras held the treaty to be in force and directed that the revenues of Guntoor should be employed in the maintainance of the troops. Even when in December, Basalat Jang represented the necessity he was under, of requiring the restoration of Guntoor, for fear of the resentment of the Nizam and Haider, the Committee refused to comply with the demand saying that the Circar had been ceded by his voluntary offer and everything had been concluded in proper order.

The time had come when Nana's efforts were to bear fruit. The dissatisfation of the Nizam exceeded all bounds. He first openly declared his sentiments to Mr. Holland and then reiterated them in a letter to the Governor-General, in which he accused the English of violating the treaty and stated that he was prepared for all eventualities. "I have therefore determined" he wrote to Nana, "as soon as the rains are at an end, I will send a distinguished chief with a resolute army and good train of artillery, or if I find it possible, I will repair in person to you and rouse that bad race from the dream of security, and overthrow all their ambitious designs. You will therefore depend on my friendship for Pundit Purdhan (i. e. the Peshwa) which is universally known." Haider found himself in a difficult situation. He could not fight the Marhattas and tbe English at once. If he wished to take his vengeance upon the English, he must make peace with the Marhattas. Nana welcomed his co-operation. Haider's agents arrived with offers of friendship,

He offered 40 lacs to settle the arrears and 11 lacs as annual Peshcush for the future. He also promised to restore the country he had wrested from the Marhattas.

Goddard's Negotiations

Nana at the same time had been carrying on negotiations with Goddard whom we left at Surat. At first Goddard's only hope lay in the dissensions which, he was informed, existed among the principal leaders of the Marhatta State. The question, how to dispose of Raghoba, required a solution when in the month of June he suddenly escaped from the custody of Scindhia. He fled to Surat taking along with him his child and his adopted son; and threw himself on the protection of Goddard. Goddard guaranteed his safety and determined to use him as an instrument in the negotiations. Nana was greatly incensed at the conduct of Scindhia in taking so little precaution to secure the person of Raghoba.

The ministers manifested an earnest desire for peace, and at the request of Goddard sent an agent to adjust all differences. In the meantime Nana's preparations for war and his solicitude to procure the assistance of neighbouring powers led Goddard to suspect his sincerity.

The agent arrived at Surat in the month of August. Goddard insisted on the repudiation of the convention. The agent naturally asked if the seal of the Company was sacred or not; Mr. Carnac had the seal and signed the convention. Goddard replied that the Bengal Govt. could not consistently with the honour and dignity of the English name, consent that a treaty solemnly entered into and regarded as an inviolable compact should be set aside without their sanction and authority. "Upon this" says Goddard in his letter of 16th August "the Vakeel pertinently remarked, that his master could not help being of opinion from what had formerly happened when the Bombay Govt: possessed themselves of Salsette, and the arguments now used, that, had the late attempt proved successful, a very different judgment would have been passed on their conduct." General Goddard laid down that the acceptance or refusal of this preliminary article was to be the sole condition of the further progress of the negotiations. The question was referred to Poona. There being some delay in the reply, Nihalchand (asstt. to the agent) himself repaired to the Marhatta capital. In October Goddard learnt that all rivalry between Nana and Scindhia had disappeared, and both were busily engaged in hostile preparations, Nihalchand returned on 28th October. Nana had refused to listen to the proposal unless Salsette was restored and Raghoba delivered over to the Marhattas. The conference broke up.

Moodajee's Dewan Dewagur was still in Poona. He seems to have been always sincerely attached to the English. He feared the Poona Durbar and stood in great awe of the great Poona statesman. He saw that right was on the side of the Poona ministers. Even in his letters to the Governor General and Goddard he admitted that the English had been guilty of breach of faith; and insisted that as the Marhatta ministers were inclined to peace, the matters should be accommodated in an amicable manner. His appeals were fruitless. Nana called upon him to join a coalition against the English to make up for his past delinquiency in allowing Goddard a safe passage through his territory. Thus under pressure brought to bear on him by both the Nizam and the Durbar he consented to become a party to the coalition; and agreed to raise an army and march towards Bengal within six weeks to lay waste the whole of that province in pursuance of the common object.

General Goddard communicated to the Select Committee of Bombay on 30th September that the ministers and Scindhia in conjunction with Haider, Nizamali, and Moodajee Bhonsla meant to make a general attack upon the English at their several settlements; and had entered into and sealed written agreements for that purpose. The great coalition was formed.

The author of the Confederacy.

The question as to who was the real author of the Confederacy assumed great importance on account of the complications which arose from it. Haider's invasion very nearly destroyed the British power in Southern India. The Governor-General attributed this invasion to the con. federacy; and the formation of the confederacy to fhe Nizam. The alienation of the Nizam was principally due to certain acts of the President and Council of Fort St. Geoge. By a logical sequence, the future writers were induced to throw the whole blame of the confederacy on Thomas Rumbold, President of the Council of Madras. Rumbold's daughter, desirous of clearing her father's reputation from the stigma attached to it by the historians, devoted many years of her old age to the study of the original records. and brought a number of new facts to light. A perusal of her work produced a complete change in the opinion of historian Marshman, and he remarked that that chapter of Indian history had to be re-written.

Haider's invasion was no doubt due to his adhesion to the coalition. But the Nizam took very little part in the formation of it. His own confession was due partly to his boastful character and partly to the desire of securing certain advantages for himself. He avowed to Mr. Holland that he had declared his intention of attacking the Cicacol and Rajmundry Circars, in case the English persisted in refusing to satisfy him with respect to the Peshcush and Guntoor affair. The Poona ministers, who had for a long time been his allies, had used every means when they knew he was discontented to incite him to join them, but without effect. Mr. Holland himself thus affirmed in another letter: "When Moodajee applied to him to know whether he might join the ministers without any danger to his dominions from the Nizam, he having suffered a great indignity and injustice by our measures, we might well suppose that he should naturally have been more inclined at such crisis to unite with our ememies than to restrain them from what their quarrels might dictate." Being, however, always in the hope of receiving satisfaction from the English he remained passive and did not move his finger to help the cause. The only thing which he can be supposed to have done, was to effect a reconciliation between Haider and the Poona ministers, as the Governor General siad, "he had avowed himself to be the adviser of the confederacy." But the persuasion of the Nizam could not furnish Haider with a motive sufficiently strong to undertake the invasion of the Carnatic. We have seen and it was rightly asserted by the Govt: of Madras, that the only obstacle in the way of Haider's carrying out his threat of war into execution, was his quarrel with the Marhattas. When Nana found that peace with the English was impossible, he at once made up the dispute with Haider; and the invasion of the Carnatic was the result. If any single person could claim to be the author of this coalition, it was Nana. Hastings himself wrote in January 1780, "The minister has been very active in his intrigues with the other chiefs of India, and it was at one time reported that he had engaged Haider, Nizamali, Nujaff Khan and even Moodajee against us. The report was not without foundation. Haider has made peace with the Marhattas, and the Nizam has conplained to this Govt: against the Presidencies of Madras and Bombay."

Hastings, position was very delicate. He was hemmed in by enemies in the Council and at home. He had to act and did act like an independent ruler. But he knew that he held a subordinate position and could be removed from his place at any time. He thus developed a natural weakness for laying the blame of a failure on some-one else. In this case, this habit led him into an error. Under the influence of that weakness he appears to have sincerely believed that the Nizam's displeasure was at the root of the Carnatic war; and that those who gave offence to the Nizam, were responsible for the calamity.

The attempt was most serious to the interests of England in India. The condition of England was critical in Europe. England stood completely isolated in the world and was confronted by the united arms of France, Spain and America. Under such an appalling aspect, the crisis in India might well be over-looked at the time. The period however has been passed over rather quietly by the historians. The public gaze was so much rivetted by cases of individual injustice which had attracted an unusual attention in England, that the real character of the period was entirely forgotten. When we enter upon a survey of the period, we have to encounter such voluminous records of the trial, the crimes, and charges against Hastings, that the mind is lost in them, and one can not understand the nature of the crisis through which the British power in India was passing,

French Intrigues, the root Cause

This coalition was the most formidable combination formed against the English in India. The design of a coalition of all the powers for the expulsion of the English was a European idea; and we therefore find it not only to have been suggested by the French agents but as being the direct object of their intrigues. By the end of the year 1777, the Nabob of Arcot had informed the Governor-General that the French had envoys at the Court of the Nizam, and Haider as well as with the Marhattas, and by means of their connection with these several powers, were trying their best to bring them round to their views. But the idea would never have taken shape if a universal alarm had not been excited by the aggressions of the English. The one thing that led all the different powers to make common cause against them, was a general impression that the English were a people who did not remain faithful to their treaties. They made treaties and violated them the moment they found it to their advantage to do so. The recent breach of the convention with the Marhattas was the most noticeable instance of it. The idea that the English were aliens, did not exercise much influence on the Indian powers. Before his inroad into the Carnatic, Haider wrote to the Governor General, "My faith that the treaties and engagements were inviolable, was illfounded. What dependence therefore can be placed upou the chiefs of the Company ? Do you however act as seems best to you." "The friendship and faith to their treaties in the English Company" saĩd Nizamali "have been from the beginning, the admiration of all the rulers; and I after 1768 found this maxim of the whole world to be true. But of late many evident infringements of the treaty should have arisen, is a matter of the greatest astonishment to anyone who reflects on the former alliances." "It is from his new line" he continued "of the conduct of the Company that the foundations of enemity have been laid in the whole country of Hindustan. If your views are hostile, lose no one in pretences, but write to the Council of Madras what a proper." Nana perhaps had a sounder view. He believed that by such means, the English wanted to create dissensions along the country powers and subdue them one after another.

Haider's Manifesto.

If we look at the language which the allies employed, we find how keenly they had determined upon the expulsion in the English from India. Before he took up arms, Haider argued a general manifesto addressed to all the Rajas, nabobs, Princes, and all the people of India. "The English nation" it began "on account of their former good faith, humanity and justice, were suffered to reside in differen parts of this Continent: permitted to carry on trade and commerce and allowed to establish factories. But our generosity have lately drawn out persons of a very differen caste who have plundered all the country of Hindustan and are making every power their tributary." Then Haidu appealed to the people against the greed, avarice and violence of the English. He said that they were attempting to hire forces to spread death and devastation, and to raise themselves to Imperial dignities "On our ruins." "If we not. my countrymen! Unite our interests and drive away the infamous invaders of our rights and properties, we have nothing to expect but one by one to fall viciims to the avarice and ambition." "If we join our forces and interes, our numbers are infinitely superior to any, the British nation can bring into the field to their support. The diff-culties that we can throw into their way, by cutting off the provisions and supplies, will soon put all their fortifications into our hands without the risk of storming them." The he goes on to describe the differences among them. "The divisions among them here are great; their wars with France Spain, and their own friends in America, will prevent England from sending any large armaments to the assistancse these wicked oppressors." He concludes by an appeal "Let us therefore not hesitate a moment, nor give these monsters in human form an opportunity to stir up dissussions among us. Let us pledge our honour and all that sacred to warriors to drive away for ever these complete enemies, robbers and disturbers of mankind and set example worthy of men and Princes."

Nujuff Kahn had his own grievance. The English had for several years past, stppped payment of the anaual tribute to the Emperor. He now saw that the opportunity of re-establishing the Imperial Supremacy over Bengal and the other Provinces had come. He wrote to the Nizam appealing to him to follow the example of his illustrious ancestors to support the dignity of the Imperial House and to render active assistanee to the alliance that had been formed against the English. In a long reply the Nizam explained to the Imperial Minister the important part he had taken in the formation of the Confederacy. He painted out how he had stirred up the Poona ministers and Haiderali Kban against the English; how the Almighty God had been pleased to infuse His-Divine light into him and by inspiration show him the way to punish those people, through whose turbulence the world was involved in calamities. "The deceits of this wicked nation" he went on "are spread over the whole Empire. Wherever the seed of their malignity has been sown, it has shortly grown up into a tree bearing the fruit of their wickedness. These people with the greatest inward deceit and treachery under the cloak of sincerity and professing a strict adherence to their engagements, have stretched forth their hands over what they in a most humble manner at first affected to borrow. A handful of people without a head or formation have possessed themselves of the three richest provinces of the Empire. A set of merchants who in their nature are like foxes, have pretended themselves on a footing with tigers." Then he explains the cause. "We owe this to our misfortunes and sins. The almighty changes not the situation of men until they change it by their own actions." "It will be difficult to root them entirely unless a resolution takes place to attack them from all quarters at once ; for if the fire of war is not lighted at the very foundation of this people, their settlements cannot be finally destroyed." Therefore "all of us have agreed to make war and peace with the concurrence of each other, that neither of the parties should suffer any loss or get any advantage without the others sharing in it." And he then in conclusion appeals to him to lead the expedition against Bengal ; "Moodajee's forces are employed to invade Bengal ; but they are not very considerable. It would be proper to send his Majesty's army to the number of two hundred thoutand horse via Lucknow into Bengal and join with Holkar and Scindhia for that purpose. Let no one have the leading of this expedition but yourself ; and embrace the opportunity of establishing the Imperial authority and power of His sacred Majesty."

Nana's Letter

Nana's letters to Scindhia are similarly filled with expressions that the English desired the ruin of all these kingdoms and their subjugatson to themselves by setting one against the other. Such were the feelings that were shared by all the leading powers of the country. This was the new danger "which.' as Burke expressed it "by a sort of miracle united the most discordant powers for our destruction, as a nation in which no other could put any trust and which was the declared enemy of the whole human species."

All the Princes came to the conclusion that the English wanted to subdue them by dividing them. They determined to crush the English by uniting, and the coalition was the result. The coalition was an assertion of the power of the Princes. It failed and the attempt was never repeated. A similar crisis occurred 78 years afterwards due to an assertion of the power of the army. The Princes believed that the English were absorbing province after province by sowing dissensions among them; and that by means of a combination they could stop the process. A similar idea made the army think that the English had conquered the country through its help; and that if the army were to rise in rebellion, the English power would he crushed to pieces.

Both cases were equally misunderstood. It was not the Indian army that had eonquered India for the Englisb. It was not the Princes who made the grants of territory to them.

It was mere force of character and superior skill and diplomacy which enabled them to use both the Princes and the army as tools to gain their ambitious ends, that the English came to possess India. The Princes, though united, were wanting in necessary strength of character and diplomacy. They could not succeed, just as the army, lacking the same requisites, failed afterwrds. The superior intellect, which could use tbem as instruments, knew also how to control them and was in the long run victorious,

The Dissolution.

"It is seldom that we see Kings and Senates avoiding the timid paths which have led others to destruction, and boldly following up through danger if necessary, a direct and manly line of honourable policy. On the contary fear makes them ingenious in self-deception and they adopt for cowardice, unwise as well as unworthy measures which sophistry represents as the dictates of absolute wisdom and of fearless liberality. History shows from first to last how certain of ruin it is to yield a single step to grasping and powerful ambition in the vain hope of courting safety by submission; and yet is there hardly an instance, recorded of men having cordially joined hand in hand to meet the threatened danger while it could be opposed to advantage." An obscure writer.

Elements of Weakness in the Coalition.

The coalition thus formed was a unique combination. There had been nothing like it in the previous history of India. The contracting parties did not therefore possess the wisdom born of experience and were ignorant of the conditions of success. Indeed it contained elements of weakness from the very beginning. No definite object was kept in view, The expulsion of the English from India, the declared aim of the allies, was too vague a thing to bind the interests of all the parties. Again it was a purely destructive work. There was no constructive programme and the parties were not promised definite advantages which could impel them to earnest endeavours on behalf of the common cause. Nobody knew what was to become of the territory, when taken out of the control of the English. In fact Moodajee and the Nizam did not believe that they could gain any advantage by destroying the power of the English. They simply looked to securing some advantages for themselves by humiliating that power. Moodajee joined the coalition in order to claim the honour of a mediator afterwards. The object which Dewagur Pundit, had in his heart, was to use this combination as a mere threat to iuduce the English to acceed to a general peace and then wait for a favourable opportunity to carry out their joint designs. He thus meant to establish his credit with the ministers and to unite the English in closer friendship with the State of Nagpore.

His double dealing is clearly proved by the fact that from the very beginning he communicated all the plans of the allies to Hastings, at the same time offering explanations of his own conduct and movements. The close relations of Hastings with the Raja of Berar were of immense service to him in this crisis. His professions of friendship had made a deep impression on Moodajee. We shall see how in the midst of all his difficulties, Hastings could always rely on him and his confidence was not misplaced.

The Nizam was dissatisfied with the English for his own affairs. He lost all interest in the coalition when he found that the English were ready to make amends in their behaviour.

Haiderali and the Marhatta ministers alone saw the real danger of English aggression and were determined to fight to the bitter end.

War Renewed.

On the breaking up of the conference at Surat, the Governor General and Council took upon themselves the responsibility of the war. In their directions to Goddard who was now made General, they wrote on 24th January 1780, that they considered Raghoba as a mere instrument whom they could not suffer to be a chargeable one. "We are determined" they say "to stand forth as principals in the war and to maintain that character through the whole course of it; as the ministers by rejecting the terms of accommodation which we proposed to them, have in effect made us so." As soon as the negotiations were at an end, Goddard set out for Bombay. The Bombay Presidency inspite of their disatisfaction with the powers granted to Goddard, showed their confidence in him by cordially promoting the success of his measures. They held their force in readiness and despatched their vessels to bring re-inforcements from Mahe. The select committee was however averse to commencing the operations on account of want of money,and of their inability to raise funds adequate to the exigencies of a war. After some discussion it was agreed to begin the operations in such a way as to secure an immediate territorial revenue, both to reimburse the Presidency for past expenses and to provide for the future exigencies of the service. The victim of these designs was Futteh Singh Gaicwar. The province of Gujrat with its divided Govt: offered an easy prey to an invader, and Goddard decided not to wait any longer. He immediately offered his conditions of alliance to Futteh Singh and advanced with his army to ensure their favourable reception. On June 2nd, he crossed the Taptee. Futteh Singh wavered for a time. On the reduction of the Fort of Dhubhoy, within a few miles of Baroda on 19th, he decided to accept the alliance on 26th January, The Marhatta forces did not arrive in time to preserve the Gaicwar to their cause. Scindhia in secret letters reproached him for the unnatural connection with the English who were enemies of the Marhatta name, and despatched a Brahman to appeal to him in the name of religion. But the Gaicwar was cowed: he could not listen to the appeals, with English guns thundering near his capital.

The Province of Gujrat was held under a joint rule between the Gaicwar and the Poona Durbar. The alliance declared that the Poona ministers were enemies of Futteh Singh and had incurred the just resentment of the English. The Durbar was therefore deprived of the share of their Govt: in Gujrat, which was made over to the English. The English thus got territory yielding a revenue of 30 lacs. Futteh Singh further promised to raise an army to support the war.

Goddard then moved towards Ahmadabad; carried it by storm on 15th February ,and according to the conditions of the allience put Futteh Singh in possession of it. In the meantime, Scindhia and Holkar who were marching with an army of 40.000 men to the help of Futteh Singh, finding that their endeavours to alienate him from the English were fruitless, turned towards Surat. Goddard hastened to intercept their march and reached Bodera on the 8th March. Here he received letters from Farmer and Steward, the two hostages who were now set at liberty by Scindhia, desiring an accomodation with the Marhatta chief. Some letters containing friendly professions passed between Scindhia, and Goddard. Scindia's object was to obtain possession by any possible means of, Raghoba and his son before entering on further negotiations. The proposal was rejected by Goddard and so the affair ended.

Scindhia avoided an open action. Though Goddard gained a slight advantage, his designs were frustrated by the extraordinary vigilance of Scindhia. Nothing of importance took place for some time except that a Bombay detachment took Callian, Bellapore and Panwelli on the coast and considerably strengthened the defence of Bombay; while a Marhatta party under Gauri Punt, committed ravages in the neighbourhood of Surat and gave some alarm to the garrison.

The Madras detachment under Col: Brown joined Goddard in the middle of April. Goddard's heart was now set on attacking Bassein. But Scindhia was lying in his way. He had ordered all the country to be laid waste so as not to leave a single blade of grass. Goddard thus finding his march blocked by this manouvre, marched back to Baroda on 9th May. He soon had to return to check the advance of Scindhia against the Fort of Dhubhoy. Slight skirmishing went on. On 22nd May, Major Forbes surprised a party of the Marhatta army. Lt: Col: Welsh attacked Ganesh Punt, and about 100 Marhattas were killed in the action. On 9th June, Welsh took Parnero, Prizen Gurh and Chandergurh; and this put the English in possession of 150 miles along the coast from Decambait to Dumaun.

In the eyes of the Bombay Govt: these successes were not satisfactory as the chief results of the campaign; because Goddard had failed in his main object of taking Bassein.

Scindhia's own country was left exposed and almost defenceless towards the North. In June he marched back to Ujjain. Goddard retired to Surat. The first campaign thus came to an end without any decisive result being achieved by either side.

Dewagur's letter to Hasting thus briefly expressed the result of the war. "Goddard writes of his victories and Scindhia and Holker talk of their own successes. Which of these accounts are we to suppose true and which false? Wherever there is war, there is likewise falsehood. Nothing but losses and disadvantages are to be expected from it."

Alliance with the Rana of Gohud.

On the close of the campaign, Goddard wrote to the Governor general suggesting a diversion in the Malwa which would detain Scindhia and Holkar for the defence of their own dominions.

The Governor General had long before been looking for an alliance in this quarter and had succeeded in securing the Rana of Gohud for the purpose.

The Rana was a bold and enterprizing soldier. He maintained perfect order and discipline in his army. He had not submitted to the authority of Nujaff Kahn. He had hitherto resisted the attacks made upon him by the Rajputs and the Marhattas. As early as 1776, out of fear of the probable attacks of the Marhattas, he had sent a request to the Governor General for military assistance and expressed his readiness to agree to such terms as might be intimated to him. The request was not granted at that time. In November 1779, when the hope of peace with the Marhattas was as distant as ever, the Governor-General laid before the Board, the draft of a treaty with the Rana in the following words: "If the war had taken place or shall take place with the Marhatta State, the treaty secures us the support and assistance of a powerful prince whose dominions adjoin to our frontier and lie in one of the principal roads through which the Marhattas must pass to invade us. At the same time, the principal in the treaty with us is a man on whose personal interest or enemity to the Marhattas, we may depend for his faithful adherence to it, He succeeded to his present dominions by the death of his father who lost his life and the fortress of Gwaliar at the same time, in an engagement with the Marhattas, with whom the son has been ever since in a state of warfare." After much discussion, the draft was agreed to by the majority on December 2nd, and Captain Palmer was deputed to the Rana for exchanging the ratification of it. On December 6th, a letter from Sir Eyre Coote, the commander in chief, who was on tour, brought intelligence of a Marhatta irruption into the Rana's territory. The Governor General thought that it was a prelude to a general attack on the company's possessions and advised that the detachment which had just then been prepared under Captain Popham to reinforce Goddard, could be more usefully employed on this side of the Jumna. In February 1780, Captain Popham was ordered to join the Rana to act against the Marhattas. Captain Popham met with some obstacles in taking the Foat of Lohar. Sir Eyre Coote, who was not in favour of the alliance, was filled with great apprehensions. He believed that the plan of action was quite unsuited to the situation. He was however completely assured when in the beginning of May, Captain Popham captured the Fort. It made him urge on vigorous exertions with a view to make a diversion to favour Goddard's operations in Gujrat The Governor General at this time had recommended some steps towards a peace with the Marhattas through the mediation of the Raja of Berar. He now suggested the necessity of improving their pretentions to better terms by an interval of successful exertion in the war and proposed that Captain Popham's detachment be reduced into three regular batallions and added to the three batallions under Major Camac: and the whole army to be supported out of the contributions of Raja Cheyt Singh,

The instructions to Major Camac were made a subject of keen contest between the Governor General and his opponents in the Council. Francis strongly objected to them as giving undue latitude to Camac to carry the Company's arms wherever he liked. The Governor-General defended the object of the expedition as being to divert the Marhatta strength. and to make the principal agent of the war suffer by it; "which" he said "was the only means to bring about an ultimate peace as the war could not be concluded honourably or prosecuted successfully with feeble measures." The Governor General now had lost his majority vote on account of the departure of Mr. Barewell to England in the month of March. He therefoee appealed to the opposition in the following manner, "The part which the Government has hitherto borne in the war, is mine, and has been made exclusively mine, the other members having repeatedly disclaimed their share in the responsibility attending it. It is hard that while they load me with the weight of such a charge, they should bind my hands and deny me the means of supporting it."

The Duel.

Francis wanted the whole plan to be laid before the Board. Hastings was enraged and in a long minute declared Francis to be void of truth and honour and by way of evidence he said, "I judge of his public conduct by my experience of his private conduct." It appears that at the time of Mr. Barewell's departure, an agreement was arranged between Hastings and Francis. The latter promised not to oppose any measure that Hastings should take in connection with the Marhatta war. Hastings then wrote it out and gave it to Francis to read. The latter read and gave his verbal approval in an indifferent manner. When the question of Major Camac's instructions came up and Francis opposed it, Hastings claimed that Francis had been false to his word and accused him of having induced him (i. e. Hastings) by a false promise of acquiescing in his measures, to part with Mr. Barewell. Francis denied having entered into any such agreement. The instructions were carried in July, Francis being absent, but Hastings would not give up the point. After some bickerings on both sides Francis simply admitted that he had given his consent to some such proposal but the expedition in question was a matter which was not at all thought of, at that time. Hastings contended that he had given the strongest demonstration of good faith by entering into such an agreement with Francis, while Francis intended to practise deception from the beginning. The dispute ultimately led to the well-known duel between them in November 1780, in which Francis was hurt, and shortly after returned to England.

Complications with the Nizam

The Board at the same time was involved in fresh complications that arose from the demands made by the Council of Madras upon the Nizam. We have seen how the resentment of the Nizam had been kindled by the proceedings of the Madras Government with regard to the Guntoor Circar. Then followed the affair of Peshcush. It should be remembered that in obeying the supplementary instructions of the Presidency, Mr. Holland exhibited a lamentable incapacity in the exercise of his discretionary power. He knew that the Presidency were not aware of the changed temper of the Nizam, when the letter applying for the remission of the Peshcush was written, so with proper reason he could withhold it. When he communicated the angry outburst of the Nizam during the conversations on the subject, the Presidency said in reply, that they wished to owe that favour entirely to the Nizam's generosity and after proposing several other alternatives, they added in the end, "Should he reject all the propositions then you must acquaint him that the Company will pay the Peshcush as soon as they are in cash."

Mr. Holland had made the mistake. He could easily have

rectified it himself, He however chose to do so by seeking the interposition of the Council of Calcutta. He wrote to Calcutta in September 1779, representing the whole case as a breach of faith on the part of his Superiors. He was deceived by the Nizam's high talk; and succeeded in impressing on the Supreme Council, the necessity of satisfying the Nizam if a crisis was to be averted. The Supreme Council at once credited his representation and offered their immediate intervention in the matter. "It is but justice" they however admitted "to acquit the[2] President and select committee of Fort St. George, of such an intention or resolution already decided within their own breasts. The contrary is evinced by their final instructions to Mr. Holland contained in their letter of 10th July. But the negotiations had led to such a state of things that they believed the interposition of the superior authority seasonable and necessary both to relieve them from difficulties and to prevent the breach."

On the first of November they wrote to Haiderali recalling all that had passed between the Nizam and Madras Govt: as being unauthorised, and at the same time, informed the Council of Madras of their resolution; and in the end referring to the demand of the remission of the Peshcush accompained with a denial of the right in a defiant tone, they concluded in the following words, "It would severely reflect on our national faith and require a long tale to which the world never attends, to convince it that the charge was without foundation; so we have judged it incumbent upon us to interfere and we have chosen such means as appeared to us likely to produce the effect." The intervention gave rise to a long and bitter dispute between the two Presidencies. It irritated the Council of Madras and hindered and delayed the settlement with the Nizam. The Council of Madras felt considerably annoyed at the tone of superiorty adopted by the Supreme Council. They asserted their equality with them, and expressed great surprise that their endeavours to relieve the company of a heavy and disgraceful burden should be interpreted as a "breach of faith." They urged that they had entered into no new treaty; they had declared no war; they had simply taken advantage of the presence of Mr. Holland at the Court of the Nizam to ask a favour; and added in the end "We are extremely concerned that you should have thought it necessary to interfere in an affair of this kind; but our feelings are still more affected by the manner in which it has been done. The proper way would have been to have allowed us to withdraw our application and not by the mode you chose to follow, which could answer no other purpose than to bring us into contempt." The reply of the Nizam was still more alarming. "The Governor of Madras had by violence" he declared "seized the Circar of Guntoor which by the treaty belonged to my brother. I was on the point of avenging them when your letter arrived. I have put a stop to my preparations. If what you write is from heart, it is well; else I have nothing of more consequence than the preserving and defending of my country; the spark of dispute and enmity will be raised to a flame." The Nizam however unwilling to enter into war, soon gave assurances of his firm friendship and steadfast adhesion to the treaty. He even agreed to give a security to dismiss the French whom he had taken into his service after their dismissal by Basalat Jang but declared that there could be no good will if the Circar was not restored. The Council of Madras would not yield an inch. In April they refused to allow Mr. Holland to continue any longer at the Court of the Nizam, and in May, ordered his suspension from office for disobedience.

Tension between Madras & Calcutta.

The Supreme Council for a time agreed to the decision of the Madras Council, but soon finding the residence of Mr. Holland indispensible, appointed him as their agent to the Court of Hyderabad. And with a view to secure the neutrality if not the friendship of the Nizam, at a period full of difficulty and hazard to the general interests of the company and the nation in India, they determined to replace everything in the state in which it was before the negotiations were entered into. In June they formally notified the resolutions to the Nizam,and required immediate compliance on the part of the Madras Govt:. The latter wanted to evade compliance as far as they could do so with impunity. They told the Superior Board that the Circar had been rented to the Nabob of the Carnatic and that they would inform the Board as soon as they heard from the Nabob. On receiving another letter from Mr. Holland in August, that the Nizam though he had declared his intention of making an attack on the company's possessions in conjunction with the Poona ministers, would remain on pacific terms provided satisfaction be given to him with regard to the Circar and the Peshcush, the Governor General repeated his injunctions to the Madras Council; and till the month of September though the Supreme Council had received news of the threatened invasion of Haider, they did not send any help and waited for full information. lest the reinforcements if sent to Madras might encourage them to insubordination.

In the latter part of 1779, the Council of Madras had sent Mr. Swartz to know the real intentions of Haider. Mr. Swartz found that Haider entertained hostile feelings towards the Company. They wrote to Calcutta on 30th October that a war with Haider would distress the Carnatic beyond measure. In December, they learnt that their troops were unable to march from Tellicherry on account of the disturbances of the Polygars instigated by Haider; and that a treaty had been concluded between Haider and the Marhattas. On December 30th, they again wrote to Calcutta, described their critical situation in view of Haider's intentions and military preparations, and pointed out the danger of carrying on war against two great powers while their natural enemies were watching every opportunity to harass them. The Governor General treated the alarm of the committee as the product of false apprehensions.

The early months of 1780 passed off quietly excepting a slight incident in which some Englishmen were arrested at Calicut. Mr. Gray was despatched to Haider to apply for their release. Before Mr. Gray arrived, Haider had already set them at liberty on a letter received from the Bombay committee with whom he kept a friendly correspondence. Mr. Gray met with a very unfriendly reception from Haider. All his professions of friendship and sincerity were answered by Haider with reproaches for the breaches of faith of which the Company had been guilty.

Haider's attack.

Rumbold, the President of Madras, left for England on

account of ill health. Haider remained busy with his preparations. He received from France great quantities of military stores. He was in constant intercourse with the French and through the influence of Mons. Chevalliar, late Governor of Chandernagar who possessed considerable influence at the Court of Paris, concluded a treaty with France for the invasion of the Carnatic on a condition of mutual advantages. The best policy for Haider was to keep quite. He had released the English prisoners so as not to rouse the fears of the English. In the month of July when Mr. Smith urged the Committee of Madras to shake off their supineness and meet the attack which had become inevitable, news was brought of the advance of Haider's troops to Changana, and of the plunder of Porto Novo and Conjeveram. The Committee ordered for the assembling of their troops and wrote to Calcutta, "We shall act in the best manner possible for our defence, but we fear our difficulties will be great for want of money as our ordinary supplies depend on the growing revenue which in case of invasion will fall very short."

Haider fully assured of the French support, issued his famous Manifesto; and set out on his work 'as far as lay in his power.' Prayers were offered alike in the mosques and the temples, for victory to the arms of Haider. The Nabob of the Carnatic was alarmed and wrote to Madras that his district was in danger of falling into the hands of Haider as there were no troops or garrison in a condition to oppose his numerous cavalry, and as the Killadars were dissatisfied with the Company and had sent their Vakeels to him. In August Haider took Arnee and three more ports and was within 50 miles of Madras. Hector Munro, the commander in chief of the Madras army himself took the command, issued directions to his office, and set out towards Conjiveram. At Arcot Haider learnt that Munro himself was marching towards Conjiveram where Col: Baillie was to join him after a circuitous march of 50 miles. Haider detached his son Tippu with a strong army to intercept Baillie; and himself marched to Conjiveram and on 3rd September encamped within 6 miles of Munro's army. Tippu had overtaken Baillie and continued to hover round him, cannonading from a distance without making a close attack. Haider suddenly left Munro, made a junction with his son and after a desperate fight compelled Baillie,to surrender on10thSeptember. Munro, instead of coming to his help, remained at a safe distance, and on hearing of the defeat, quietly retired. The loss of the English in killed and wounded amounted to about 400 Europeans and about so many thousand Sepoys. This was the greatest misfortune that ever befell the English in India. The Madras Govt: atonce despatched a swift vessel, Nymph, to carry the intelligence to Calcutta. The Council now saw the need of conciliating the Nizam. On September 14th, they wrote to Captain Douglas to make over the Guntoor Circar to Basalat Jang, and a few days after sent a letter to the Nizam lamenting their inability in paying the arrears of the Peshcush due for the other Circars; but desiring him to believe their assurances that they would neglect no opportunity, for the future, of making good their balances. They concluded with a confident hope that His Highness would act according to the treaties subsisting between them and endeavour to the utmost of his powers to check the designs of their enemies.

The Nizam was pacified. He declared to Mr. Holland that the conduct of the English was always influenced by the spirit of amity, and that they would surely redress the injury he had suffered for the last 15 months. The sudden success of Haider had excited the N zam's jealousy. From that moment he wavered between his jealousy of Haider and his dread of violating his faith with the confederates. Now he lost all interest in the confederacy and thus one member of the coalition was alienated. Mr. Hollaud wrote in December "His Highness holds friendly disposition to us though he is secretly encouraging Haider, even with promises of an army. I am clearly of opinion that it would be unsafe at any time so far as to rely on his friendship as to be off our guard or to trust him further than his own interests might warrant our confidence."

Helplessness of Madras.

Madras was helpless. The alarming superiority of Haider and the news of the French armament which was expected to come to his help, threw the English into the utmost consternation. In the face of these dangers, the Supreme Council laid aside every other consideration and exerted itself with might and main to avert the crisis. The Governor General appealed to the zeal of the Commander in chief, and asked him to take the command in person to retrieve the disgrace and to preserve the interests of his country from utter ruin. He further proposed that an immediate peace should be offered to the Marhattas through Moodajee on condition that the situation existing before the war should be restored and provision should be made for Raghoba. These terms were to be offered if the Peshwa was prepared to join in an offensive and defensive alliance against Haiderali; otherwise a truce for one year in order to settle terms of peace, was to be concluded on the condition that each party should retain the conquests made during the war. It was believed that the victory of Haider must have made the Marhattas jealous of Haider and would induce them to wish for a connection with the English.

Had Haider followed up his success, he would have been master of Madras. Instead of marching upon Mardras, he turned to Arcot, the capital of the province, to the capture of which he attached great importance. From a military point of view, this is said to have been the greatest mistake made by Haider. In one way it was so, Haider lost sight of the fact that the English were masters of the Sea and in a little while, could bring a fresh army from Bengal. But there is this thing to be said in his favour. He knew that there was a coalition and that he had played his part by completely crushing the Engligh power in the South. Had Moodajee done his duty, Bengal would have been in a similar predicament and too much occupied at home to send any help to Madras. He could have no knowledge of the lukewarnness of the Raja of Berar.

Lukewarmness of Moodajee.

We have seen that Dewagur Pundit had joined the coalition and had promised to raise an army for the invasion of Bengal. Consequently in January 1780, an army of thirty thousand Marhattas was despatched towards Bengal under the command of Moodajee's son, Chimnajee. Dewagur however assured the Governor-General that that was done simply to keep up appearances ; and offered his mediation for a general peace. The march of the troops was purposely protracted till the season for action was over. Governor-General himself explained the real motives of the Raja of Berar in answer to a question put by Sir Eyre Coote in the Council. He told the Council that Moodajee had cheerfully complied to permit the detachment to pass through his territory offering free passage and subsistence. He had readily advanced money to Goddard due on his bills though Goddard marched to Bombay against his remonstrances. He had given another proof of friendship in helping Mr. Elliot to obtain the surrender of M. Chevalliar at Cuttack. "His disposition" he continued, 'is still the same. All their movements have been previously and confidentially communicated to this Government, The Diwan was despatched to Poona, their Government having been exposed to the resentment of the Poona Durbar, to negotiate a peace with Goddard. He failed in the attempt. He communicated to me every circumstance that happened during his stay there. It was from him that I heard of the Confederacy planned by the Nizam and formed in conjunction with the minister at Poona and Haider against the Company. He was called upon by the minister to furnish his quota of troops for the cause and threatened by the Nizam and Scindhia that they would invade and lay waste his country if he refused. He was totally unprepared to resist two such formidable enemies and was obliged to enter into the general confederacy. The part assigned to him, was to send an army to lay waste the province of Bengal; but he informed me that he should continue such means of delay as should prevent the army from approaching our borders till the close of fair season which would be a plea for not entering into immediate action, This declaration has been literally verified, for we have seen this body of troops spin out a march to four months which might with ease have been accomplished in two ; and arrive at the place of their destination, at the commencement of the rains. These, though Marhattas, have remained as quiet as though cantoned at their own capital. Every letter from the Court of Berar is filled with the most solemn assurances of actual friendship and his resolution to maintain it. It is their earnest wish and ambition to become the mediator and guarantee of peace ; and it is my firm conviction that if it shall fail of its purpose and he compelled to take a decided part in the war. he will rather unite with us than to submit to act with his natural enemies." The letters from the Raja and Dewagur Pundit which are numerous, are filled with sincere regard and friendship for the English. "The authority, greatness, power aud strength of the gentlemen" rnns a passage in one of the Raja's lettors to Beneram "were like a river that has large waves but from their great and striking virtues, their piety and love of God, they go not beyond the boundaries fixed by their treaties and engagements, and if at any time in their intercourse of friendship, events and circumstances, any difficulties should come upon their friends, they like a river which supports upon its waters, the great weight of large ships, take upon themselves the weight of them and deposit them safely on the shore." Dewagur's letters read more like dissertatlons on the evils of war; by which means he thought of persuading both sides to peace and thus have the honour of a peace maker. "It is right and proper" he wrote to

Beneram "that peace should be brought about between them by me; that I may on the side of the Marhattas have a claim on their gratitude; and on the side of the English to shall enhance our friendship with them."

Francis too admitted that the Raja's desire for peace was sincere and conformable to the language he had uniformally held. On the arrival of the army at Orissa, the Governor General treated it as friendly, and ordered supplies of grain to relieve its distress. The army was maintained at a greay expense. The lowest estimate was 9 lacs of Rs a month By September it had cost nearly a crore (hundred lacs) of Rs, paid solely out of the Nagpore treasury.

Already in the month of June, the Dewan had hinted that the English ought to share the burden with Nagpore. Its September, he instructed Beneram to make a secret demand of 16 lacs for the expenses of the army; and added "Let not the Governor General apprehend that this money will be thrown away; for the Bhonsla and the English interests will be one and much benefit will flow from it. To bring this about, with extreme secrecy is necessary, extremely necessary. I do not want it for myself. This is the advice to be followed most certainly, or the army will be no longer governable. If the army remains till the months of Pool and Magh (corresponding to December and January), they fear of the English will be upon all and therefore this ought to be effected." The Governor General secretly sent 3 lacs to Chimnajee which brought a little relief; but the Dewali continued to press for a more adequate contribution.

When the Governor General made the proposal of peace with the Marhattas through Moodajee, the Council sommoness

Beneram for examination. He declared that Moodajee needed 15 lacs for the supplies of the troops. That his master had pledged his faith before God that his troops would not cross the Company's territory or act against the English. He further affirmed that if the terms offered through Moodajee. were not accepted by the Peshwa, he should become an open ally of the Company; that the reputation of the Bhonsla family was a sufficient guarantee of his words, "as never was any ancestor of this family accused of neglect or breach of faith in his promises with whomsoever entered into by oaths or engagements."

On October 2, the terms of the treaty accepting Moodajee's mediation, were passed and signed for transmission to Nagpore. Letters to the same effect were written to the Peshwa, Scindhia and to the Nizam. The Supreme Council at the same time passed an order for the suspension of Mr. Whitehill, the President of Madras for showing a complete disregard of the orders of the SupremeCouncil and for offering an insult to their diginity. This fact is not of any importance except that it showed how the Governor General vented his wrath on the Councii of Madras and that accordingly it misled the historians to suppose that it compelld the Council of Madras to restore the Circar of Guntoor to the Nizam.

Sir Eyre Coote Leaves for Madras

The nexst day Sir Eyre Coote embarked for Madras with 320 European artillery, 630 lascars and some guns. Fifteen lacs were sanctioned to provide them with supplies.

The power over sea was a great bond of union among the distant English settlements. When Calcutta was taken, Madras sent an army to retake it. Now Madras was in danger, Bengal supplied all recources and saved it. All the settlements were like the roots of a great tree, so they not only supported the tree but supplied food to each other. Wherever one spreading root met an obstacle, there they gathered all their strength and employed all available resources.

In the way Coote observed the effect which the success of Haider had produced on the native army. At Vizigapatam, three batallions had risen in mutiny on 3rd October, killed several Englishmen, made the chief a prisoner, and declared their owu Nabob.

On landing he found to his great mortification that the country both to the north and the south was in flames. There were not supplies enough for a month in Madres; "We depend on Bengal for everything" he wrote" the country around us affords us no assistance." The first thing he had to do, was to carry out the orders for the suspension of Mr. Whitehill. A strange scene took place in the Counil. Mr. Whitehill was determined not to submit to 'the unjust and unauthorised interference.' He argued that the charges had lost all the foundation at the time they were framed, and that they were based on acts for which he alone was not responsible. It was with great difficulty that Whitehill was forced to vacate his place.

Haider had been beseiging Arcot, the capture of which added twenty thousnd men to his troops. This dissatisfied the Madras Sepoys very much, a large number of whom had their wives and children in Arcot. It also created in them a kind of aversion to serving under the English which resulted in many desertions. No one could be trusted. Coote suffered from another disadvantage. Haider's cavalry covered all the roads and he had cut off the English from all sources of informatin. As a proof, wrote Coote on his arrival, it was thonght that Arcot was in the possession of the Engliah, while in fact it had fallen two days before he reached Madras. But above all, what struck most powerfully at the root of the English influence, was in the opinion of Sir Eyre Coote, the fact that Haider immediately after taking Arcot, proclaimed protection to all the inhabitants and strictly forbade their being plundered or in any way molested. Some of his troops who entering the town began to plunder, were instantly seized and beheaded. Such scrupulous regard for the life and property of the inhabitants as well as his assumption of tbe title of the Soubah, secured to him the submission of all the Polygars and the collectors of the Nabob. They all attended on Haider and were confirmed by him in their places.

The keen eye of Haider had picked up carefully all the points in which lay the superiority of the English. What with his military organisation and what with his political insight, he was a product of the English system, every inch a pupil of the English.

In November, the French at Pondicherry rose in arms, robbed the Resident and forced him at the point of the bayonet, to sign a paper, the contents of which he did not understand. They then burnt the English flag and raised 1000 Sepoys, and 100 Topazas. The French fleet was not very distant on its way to Pondicherry. The fortress of Gingee was in the enemy's hands. Wandwash and Parmacoil were beseiged. The enemy's horse made its appearance daily in one quarter or another. The scarcity of provisions continued in Madras. For nearly a month the Europeans had not even one full meal a day. "I never experienced,' wrote Sir Eyre Coote "So many difficulties and failures in the execution of duties. I am cruelly detained for want of carriage for the provisions and stores, every grain of which, I am under the necessity of carrying from hence." Then he was informed that Nana was not inclined to an alliance with the English. He was averse to deserting Haider. He had directed Haider's Vakeel to inform his master that he was his firm friend, and had written to Moodajee to intercept the detachment proceeding from Bengal; and Haider could therefore proceed to conquest in confidence. "I declare it as my firm opinion" Coote thus concluded "that with present exhausted state of our finances and with so powerful a combination as has been formed against us, by the first Princes of Hindustan and with every man capable of assisting us in the Carnatic, our enemy, we are very unequal to the contest and no means should be left untried to effect an accommodation with the Marhattas, nor any pursued which may put a period to war which threatens our interests in India with irrecoverable ruin."

Anxiety of the Supreme Council.

The Supreme Council forwarded large supplies of grain and other materials to Madras. They were moreover induced to propose a treaty of alliance by offering territorial concessions to the Dutch, and despatch an envoy to Goa, to request the Portuguese Govt: that they should send a body of their forces to make an inroad into Haider's territory. They had also prepared another detachment under Col:

Pearse, to be despatched overland to reinforce Coote. The Berar troops were lying in the way, its march was therefore delayed till the arrival of the reply from Nagpore. The Supreme Council in appealing to Moodajee for mediation had entertained a hope of getting a portion of the Berar army added to Col: Pearse's detachment. The open secession of such a powerful member would have been a crushing blow to the Confederacy. The expected answer arrived on the 9th of January 1781 and greatly disappointed the Board. It contained so many objections to the terms of the proposed treaty that little hope was left of an accommodation with the Poona Govt. Though the Governer General was led for a time to doubt the sincerity of Moodajee's professions, the Board ordered the Detachment to march and sent Mr. Anderson to propose terms to Raja Chimnajee. On reaching Cuttack, Mr. Anderson found that Chimnajee had retired to the hills under the pretence of reducing the petty Rajas but his real object was to remove his army in order to afford an easy passage to the English troops. Chimnajee soon returned and recalled Mr. Anderson for the purpose of negotiating with him. Through Raja Ram Pundit, the viceroy of Cuttack, an engagement was concluded on the 29th of March, by which the Raja agreed to detach a body of 2.000 horse to be placed under Col: Pearse and to be paid by the English at one lac per month; and in return the English were to send a party of the Company's forces to assist the troops of Berar in taking from the Peshwa, a small district Guramundla, on the banks of the Nurbudda; and to grant 13 lacs, the remainder of 16 lacs for the relief of the army by way of "an acknowledgment for the past and seasonable instances of friendship afforded by the Govt: of Berar."

Though no other practical good came out of the agreement, it served as a death-blow to the Confederacy. The Governor General and Council observed with great satisfaction, "we have laboured and we think with a success now decided to detach the most poweful member of the Marhatta State; and in its relations to Bengal, the most capable of any in India to do it either service or hurt, from the general confederacy which has been formed against us, and have converted it, ostensibly at least, into a party to our cause. The event will shorty prove the truth of our conclusions." The above sum of 16 lacs is represented as a bribe, the price of Moodajee's desertion from the coalition. But the account given above is enough to show that the Dewan was from the beginning betraying the Marhatta cause. For mere show, he had exhausted the treasury of Nagpore on the maintenance of an army which did not serve any useful purpose. Till the last he remained under the impression that he had been the chief instrument in restoring peace to the benefit of all the parties and therefore it was their duty to reimburse him for the expenses incurred. "In case, peace is made 'he wrote 'something must be done by the Peshwa, something by the Nizam and something by the English to make good the expenses. Great losses and expenses have been brought on us by the raising of a new army." "Distress for money is my excuse" he said again, "else the Maharaja like others of his family. is not self-interested. Wherever they place their friendship, they do not hesitate to stake their lives, much less their fortunes, provided either can serve to promote the ends of friendship."

Coote's Operations.

The difficulties of Sir Eyre Coote continued to grow as time went by. Though expressing his satisfaction at the repeated assurances of support in money and stores, he sent his bitter protests against "a system of policy so ruinous in itself and so destructive to the interests of their employers." In the middle of January he was able to decide on the relief of Wandwash; and when he succeeded, he could say with a well-deserved pride "Twenty one years ago, I raised the siege of this place by a battle with the French." From Wandwash he set out towards Permacoil. Hearing of the arrival of the French fleet and apprehending a siege of Madras, he turned back. Again learning that the fleet had marched to Pondicherry, he resolved at all risks to march to that place. He reached there on 5th of February, but had no provisions. Haider with his cavalry was on the pursuit. On the 7th the whole of Haider's army was in sight. Coote resolved to anticipate Haider and marched towards Cuddalore. He was overtaken and after a loss of some lives by tho enemy's fire completed his march. The real difficulty was in the lack of provisions which could not last even for 3 days. The enemy occupied all the roads and destroyed all chance of drawing supplies from the country. The supplies from sea were cut off by the French fleet at Pondicherry and by armed vessels belonging to Haider, lying at Porto Novo. Yet on the very existence of this army depended the British interests in the Eastern world. The alarming prospect, produced feelings in Coot's mind which can be more easily imagined than described. "What to determine" he wrote "in a situation so critical, so difficult, and in its consequences so important, I confess, was a question I dreaded the decision of. In short I saw in the fall of this handful of men, the destruction of English interests in India." On the 10th he marched his army to offer battle. The enemy retired and moved off across the river. On the 11th he even crossed the river to tempt the enemy, but they retired and frustrated his device. The provisions were now exhausted. "In order to obtain subsistence from day to day we were obliged to send forth parties, to dig the grounds for Paddy (rice) which the inhabitants in times of trouble are apt to lay up as a security against want. By this means we obstained a little. Had it not been for the spirited exertions of Mr. Danicl who at all risks sacked the town to procure us supplies of grain, we must have been reduced to a state which forebode the most fatal consequences." The inhabitants began to starve. Sevral died of want of food, and a few days more would have completed the melancholy scene. But all this was suddenly changed by the French fleet getting under sail which opened a prospect of obtaining supplies from the north. Some vessels of rice which were waiting at Sadras, arrived on the 17th of February. Haider pressed the French admiral to stay a little longer, but all his supplications were fruitless De, orves was false to his country and reputation. "Never had France an opportunity of taking her revenge on the English for the defeats of Dupliex and Lally. There was no doubt about the issue." "I need not" says Sir Eyre Coote "take up your time with comments on the conduct of the French Admiral or in describing the injuries we must have suffered and the risk we must have run, if he had acted with common spirit; I may safely advance that we are entirely indebted to his irresolute behaviour (something worse than that) for the little security we now enjoy on that coast. He drew Haider from Arcot with strong assurances of support and when he came near, failed in the performance."

The crisis was over. Then came the important battle of PortoNavo, in which Haider suffered a defeat, from the effects of which he never recovered, even though he gainad some successes afterwards.

General Goddard received the resolution about peace when he was preparing for his second campaign. The supreme Council had instructed him to keep the resolution, an inviolable secret, and to suspend hostilities on receiving a requisition from the Peshwa to that effect; but until such requisition or notification was received he was to prosecute war with the utmost vigour.

General Goddard's failure

The Bombay Presidency had one ambition, that is,the capture of Bassein which would put them in possession of a revenue equal to their expenditure.Besides the new situation would enable them to exhibit their strength and make a war of defence easy for them, in case hostilities were continued. Bassein was therefore now the object of Goddard's operations. The Presidency had ordered the assembling of forces at Callian, the possession of which had secured for them an opening into Concan. About the middle of September, intelligence arrived at Bombay that the Portuguese were intriguing with the Poona Durbar for taking possession of Bassein and were making preparations to be beforehand with the English. The news quickened the movements of Goddard. He reached there on 13th November. On 11th December, Bassein surrendered and Goddard then repaired to Bombay to consult about further operations. The news of the disaster in the Carnatic had been received there, and now a letter from Sir Eyre Coote urged them for an invasion on Haider's territories on the Malabar coast. Tellichery attacked by a party of Marhattas and Haider's men, so long abondoned to its fate, urgently needed relief. Finally in a consultation it was agreed that a vigorous prosecution of war against the Marhattas, promised a speedy settlement, and an expeditiou on Arnoul was determined upon. The expedition was at first successful. General Goddard got possession of Boreghaut. Nana was not alarmed; he went on with vigorous preparations, and rejected all offers of peace unless Haider participated in the negotiations. Purshram with 12,000 troops was despatched to harass Goddard. The progress of Goddard towards the Ghauts was stopped by the approach of the Marhatta armies. Captain Macky's escort, bringing a convoy of grain, was surprised and so closely pursued that it was nearly all destroyed. In March Goddard decided to march backwards to Bombay. Another party under Col: Brown, bringing a convoy of grain, was attacked by Purshram and had all its cattle carried away. Col: Brown could not march till reinforcements were sent from Bombay; and then after suffering a loss of more than hundred men, he joined the main army on April 15th. The general now began his retreat. But he found himself surrounded by three great Marhatta armies; Tokajee Holkor with 15,000 men lay at the bottom of the Ghauts; Purshram with 12,000 men. below and Hurry Punt with 25,000 men ablove the Ghauts, On 20 April, Hurry Punt broke in and took away tents and a great quantity of ammunition. During the march the General was much harassed by the Marhattas and reached Panevel on the 23rd after a loss of 400 men in killed and wounded, out of which 18 were European officers. This retreat of Goddard is considered by the Marhattas as one of their most signal victories. The English army cantoned at Callian. The Marhattas retired and Goddard repaired again to Bombay. With the failure of Goddard's last expedition, the plan of bringing the war to an end by vigorous measures, had failed. Various other plans were now laid before the Bombay Council, and came under discussion. Nothing definite was determined upon till November. when news reached Bombay that peace could be hoped for from quite a different quarter.

Captain Popham's Plan.

After taking the Fort of Lahore, on 4th July 1768 Captain Popham, conceived the plan of surprising the Fort of Gwaliar, which had been pronounced by the Princes of Hindusthan to be impregnable. The enterprize was attended with enormous difficulty and danger. His success was therefore regarded as a brilliant feat of arms. The Marhattas at once retired from the country, and the achievement alarmed Scindhia in his capital. The English were proud of the conquest and seemed to consider it dishonourable to part with the Fort. Instead of handing it over to the Rana as promised in the treaty, they kept it in their hands. It was said to be "the key to Hindusthan." This circumstance not only alienated the Rana from the English and impeded the expedition but produced an alarming effect on the Court of Delhi. In spite of all the exertions of the ministers and Scindhia to bring him actively in the conflict. Nujuff in whom the Government of Delhi was vested had remained a passive sympathiser of the confederacy. The presence of a British army in the Fort of Gwaliar, was a serious menace to the Imperial Court he therefore ordered Zabita Khan at the head of 30,00,0 horse and 40,000 fighting Sikhs to proceed to Muradabad and join Scindhia's forces. Nujuff Khen however wanted both money and materials. Revenue was inadequate and want of money rendered it extremely difficult for him to execute his project. Besides, in the latter part of his life Nujuff Khan devoted much of his time to the pleasures of the harem and had lost his old reputation for energy and enterprize. He was also afraid of leaving Delhi lest his interests should suffer by the intrigues in his absence.

Major Camac's favourable reception.

In September 1780, orders had been issued to Major Camac to make a junction with the army of Popham and proceed to attack Malwa, the territory of Scindhia. Camac did not begin operations till the beginning of the following year. Scindhia meanwhile was busily engaged in gaining over all the chiefs by offering them favourable terms. A number of these Chiefs and Zamindars who had been, a short time before stripped of their possessions by the Marhattas, were disaffected towards them. This fact had assured Major Camac that he would not encounter much opposition in the conpuest of Malwa. Hostilities commenced in January 1781, with the storming of Sipree by

Johnston. The greatest injury to the cause of the Marhattas, was done by their friends, the Pindarees. The Pindarees were the pioneers of the Marbatta armies. They plundered the villages wherever they went. A number of the Zamindars from several villages in fear of the Pindarees, sought protection of the English army. "It must be a communication of the most pleasing nature to Government," wrote Camac "to know that the inhabitants of this country showed the warmest and most favourable disposition towards us. The enemy ravage and despoil their towns while we are expected and received as deliverers." These places were delivered over by Camac to the Raja of Newar who was the head of the Cuchwai tribe of Rajputs, and had shown a friendly disposition to the English. The Raja was so much pleased that he sent his own brother with troops to help the English. The prestige of his name was of great use in influencing the native mind. The Nabob of Bhopal, at the same time made a treaty with the English. Notwithstanding these advantages, the force under Camac was very inadequate and in February he applied to the Supreme Council for permission to raise six or eight hundred horse "Which" he said "I can easily do for the same or perhaps less pay than the Candhrees have with General Goddard." Soon after (end of February) he was surrounded by Scindhia's army at Serongee. He endured a cannonade for 7 days and then retreated, pursued and harassed by an army of 30,000 men. He suffered a heavy loss. The number of the wounded was so large that he did not know where to lodge them. Much of the baggage was taken by the enemy. In such a critical situation he wrote to Col: Morgan for relief, upon which Col: Muir was ordeıed to expedite his march and take the command from Major Camac. Before Muir arrived, Camac surpised Scindhia's army and took possession of several guns; and thus retrieved the disgrace which the British arms had suffered by his retreat.

Hastings was at this time thinking of starting on his journey, "the principal and ruling motive" for which expedition was in his own words "to determine Dewagur Pundit to a meeting with me". He thought it critically necessary to guard against anything which might affect the general credit of the Company's faith; and especially at a time when he was on the eve of negotiations with the Court of Berar. Consequently he ordered the restoration of the fort of Gwaliar to the Rana of Gohud. He was so far from running the risk, that he declared, "I heartily wish that the law would declare it a felony to break treaties. Nothing would contribute more to the permanency of our influence in this country." The Rana was satisfied and was now ready to co-operate with Col: Muir against Scindhia.

Scindhia was now tired of the war and inclined to come to terms. He was afraid of maintaining a contest in the heart of his country from which he had nothing to gain but much to lose. In October he agreed to the terms and guaranteed to bring about a peace with the Durbar. The Governor-General was at that time in Benares where he had received the news of Dewagur's death. He was much pleased to hear of this new opening for a general pacification. He appointed Mr. Anderson to carry on the negotiations and wrote to Col: Muir to assure Scindhia that the

English would not interfere in his designs at the Court of Delhi. Besides the pressure brought to bear upon the Poona Durbar by Scindhia, great effect was produced by a letter from Madras giving solemn assurances of peaceful intentions and sincere desire for a general peace with an open offer to yield to the demands of the Durbar.

Lord Macartney's 'offer of peace.'

By this time, Lord Macartney had come to India as Governor of Madras. He was a man possessed of unexampled purity of conduct and a spirit of rare integrity and disinterestedness. His policy in Indian affairs was to be guided by high and noble aims. "I am free to confess," he said that I have a stronger passion than the love of wealth—to reinstate India in its former glory would give me more pride and satisfaction than I should be able to derive from ten times the fortunes of Mr. Hastings." He came with his mind full of a desire for peace. It was the opinion of Admiral Edward Hughes and Sir Eyre Coote that no amount of success could carry the conflict to a favourable issue, as it was altogether in Haider's power to avoid or terminate an action whenever he pleased. With the victory of Porto-Novo, it was believed that offers of peace could be made to Haider with dignity and success. His answer however furnished a most unfortunate instance of distrust and dissatisfaction to which the former transactions had given rise. "The Governors and Sardars" he replied "who enter into treaties, after two or three years, return to Europe. Their deeds and acts become of no effect and fresh Governors and Sardars introduce new conversations. Prior to your coming when the Governor and

Council of Madras had departed from the treaty of alliance and friendship, I sent my Vakeel to complain with them and to ask the reason for such breaches of faith, the answer given was that they who made the conditions, were gone to Europe. You write that you come with the sanction of the King and the Company to settle all matters; which gives me great pleasure. You, Sir, are a man of wisdom and comprehend all things, whatever you may-judge most proper and best, that you will do. You mention that troops have arrived and are daily arriving from Europe, of this I have not a doubt. I depend upon the favour of God for my succours."

Lord Macartney was not disappointed. Early in September, a letter was addressed to the Peshwa in the joint names of Lord Macartney, Sir Edward Hughs, Sir Eyre Coote, and Mr. Macpherson through the Nabob's Vakeel at Poona, stating their wish for peace and desire of the British nation to conclude a firm and lasting alliance and treaty which no servant of the Company should have power to break, and assuring the Peshwa upon their own honour, that of the King, the Company and of the Nation that just satisfaction would be given in a sincere and irrevocable treaty. The letter produced such an effect on the Court of Poona that no hostilities were committed after this period.

Conclusion.

"It is the opinion of this Court that Warren Hastings, Governor-General of Bengal and the members of the Supreme Council have displayed uncommon zeal and ability and exertion in the management of East India Company during the late hostilities in India, particularly in finding resources for supporting the war in the Carnatic under so many pressing difficulties, when that country was in danger of being lost." The resolution of the General Court of Proprietors November 7, 1783.

Hastings attachment to Moodajee.

Thus a dreadful war, which being carried on in almost all parts of India, had entailed an enormous expenditure, was regarded by Hastings as a mere episode which did not interrupt the steady development of his vast political designs. He never lost sight of his favourite project which he described in the following words : "If ever the house of Moodajee shall assert its pretensions to the Rajya or Sovereignty of Satara, and solicit our aid to obtain it, I hope it will be granted. It will prove the most fortunate connection that was ever made by the British nation in India and properly managed may ensure its lasting dominion over the Empire virtually though not actually held." He had no reason to give up that design. In the midst of so many difficulties, Berar had remained faithful to him. Had Dewagur kept his engagement with the Poona Durbar and had the Berar army attacked Bengal, the ruin of English rule in India would have been hard to avert. It was Bengal that supplied all the sinews of war to the other two Presidencies. A perusal of Dewagur's letters shows what a spell Hastings had cast over his mind. "I look upon the Governor-General as my own master" he once wrote to Beneram, the agent of Berar in Calcutta, "and speak for his welfare." Beneram Pundit was the link between Hastings and Dewagur. Hastings thus acknowledged his services as he recommended his brother to General Goddard; "I have found him so useful and I believe him so truly attached to me that I interest myself on his brother's behalf." Next to the display of military skill, it was the personal charm of Hastings that saved the English in the crisis.

The Nizam and Haiderali

On the news of the agreement between Raja Chimnajee and the Supreme Council, Nana threatened Moodajee with the vengeance of the Peshwa's Government. This circumstance, added to the great victory over Goddard gained by the Marhatta armies prevented Moodajee from taking any active part on the side of the English. Dewagur Pundit however was preparing to have an interview with Hastings at Benares, when death overtook him. With his disappearance, the Court of Berar lost all the influence it had commanded in settling the political relations among the powers of the country.

It has already been shown that ever since the Circar was restored to the Nizam, he had lost interest in the Confederacy ; but he had abstained from openly joining the English. The Nizam always entertained a great jealousy of Haider's ambitions—a feeling which was in every way encouraged by the English. After Haider's victory, his agent at Delhi, Balmokand offered a Peshcush of 2 lacs to the Emperor for the grant of the Carnatic to his master. The agents of the Nizam, Budh Singh and Budrirow, endeavoured to counteract the success of Haider's negotiations, pleading the claims of their master for some mark of royal favour and declaring his readiness to pay a sum in excess of that offered by Haider. It was rumoured that Nujuff Khan had made a protestation of friendship with Haider (by exchanging turbans) ; and sent him a turban and Khilat (robes of honour) from the king coupled with a royal grant of the Carnatic. This report naturally excited the Nizam's jealousy to a high pitch ; and the Supreme Council's letter addressed to Mr. Holland in October 1781, served the purpose of adding fuel to the fire. "His Highness is no less distinguished" they wrote" for his wisdom and knowledge of the affairs of Hindustan and European Governments, than for his high and hereditery situation. His Highness must therefore see clearly that the great ambition of Haider and his established connection with our European enemies, render him no less an enemy to His Highness than to the English. The Sunnuds for which he has been applying openly at the Court of Delhi and his wishes to possess all the countries from the Western to the Eastern Sea, show clearly that the bounds of his ambition include the dominions of His Highness. From these considerations, so clear in themselves, it is a matter of surprise to us that a Prince of His Highness's ability has not seized the present opportunity to invade the contiguious dominions of Haider."

Fazel Khan, one of the chiefs of the Nizam, and a man possessed of great insight and political acumen, was from the beginning opposed to any connection with the English. Mr. Holland had complained bitterly of Fazel Khan's endeavours to prevent him from gaining any influence at the Court of Hyderabad. He possessed an intimate knowledge of of the secret wishes of the Nizam and guided his policy accordingly. The death of this confidential adviser at this time, left the Nizam without a guide, and he now openly espoused the cause of the English. Nana alone remained true to Haider, as the latter had been faithful to his word. He was not prepared to make peace with the English, till Haider was included in it. He made the restoration of Salsette to which he had a kind of religious attachment, the principal condition of peace.

Haider was carrying on war and had even gained several successes. But age was gaining on him. His sudden death, followed by that of Nujuff Khan soon after, which opened a new field to the ambition of Nana, brought about a change in his policy. He mourned the loss of Haider, "Oh! he was a great man", and then pressed upon Scindhia to ratify the treaty, hasten to Delhi and take possession of the Emperor's person before theEnglish arrived there. After Haider's death,his sonTippu took up the war,which after some fighting came to a conclusion in1784by the treaty of Manglore.

The Storm is Over.

The storm thus psssed away. It had been full of dangers. It might have involved the destruction of the English power in India. The failure of the Bombay expedition, Haider's formidable invasion, Goddard's successes and final retreat, English fears of the presence of the Berar army on the confines of Bengal, the threats of the Nizam, and the war in the North were not detached events, but were the consequences of one great volcanic force, the eruption of which took place in different forms and in different places. That the fury and violence of it were not fully and clearly realised either in India or in England, is due to the wonderful patience and endurance of the man who alone bore the brunt of it.

The success of Hastings against such a powerfull combination, was largely due to his diplomatic skill in breaking it up. But mere diplomacy unaided by physical force, would have effected little. It was above all his ability to prosecute the war simultaneously in so many quarters that convinced the wavering members of the Confederacy, of the impossibility of achieving success in their attempts. They withdrew from the coalition having been assured of the futility of their designs. Any display of weakness or exhaustion in the resources of his Govt: might have turned them into dangerous enemies. Yet says James Mill in his great work, "His (Hastings') friends would not affirm that the Empire would have been destroyed, had be depended on the resources, in his hands. Then all what he did, was for convenience." No view can be more superficial. It is true, the Directors never enjoined or applauded any crime. Far from it. "But whoever examines their letters written at the time. will find" says Macaulay "many just and humane sentiments, many excellent precepts,in short an admirable code of political ethics. But every exhortation is modified or nullified by a demand for money. "Govern leniently and send more money." "Practise strict justice, moderation towards neighbouring powers and send more money." This in-truth is the sum of all the instruction that Hastings ever received from home."

For war, men and money were needed. England, being involved in war with all Europe and America, was unable to send either. Men could be found in India to serve in the English army. Patriotic feeling as against the foreigner was entirely absent among the mass of the people. Whether this want of patriotic feeling was due to a highly developed civilisation or to a complete lack of the national spirit, will remain a subject of dispute. But the men must be paid. Money was the one thing needful. How to get it was the question, on a proper solution of which depended the success of the war. Hastings knew that he alone had to meet the difficulty, and find resources for it without any hope of assistance from any quarter. He found the resources, though not without having recourse to certain acts of injustice and violence. There were four different sources from which money could be obtained. First,came England.The Colonies were in revolt and the nation was engaged in war with France, Spain, and Holland. The Govt : at home were calling upon the Company for extraordinary supplies in aid of the public necessities. France sent 18 ships of the line and at least ten million sterling to her islands to be employed for the destruction of the British power in India. England sent a powerful fleet and as many troops as they could spare from the pressing demands made upon her from other quarters; but she left Hastings to find resources as best as he could for supporting 70 thousand men in the field.

Need for Money

Next source were the territorial revenues. When Hastings took charge of the Govt: of Bengal;it was loaded with a debt of one crore (ten millions) and one lac of Rs. which increased to one crore and twenty lacs a short time afterwards. Under his administration, not only was the whole of the debt paid off but a sum of 2 crores and twenty one lacs was accumulated in the treasury. The time came when difficulties set in, expenditure increased and the revenues showed a decline. From 1774 to 1779 the supplies amounted to a little less than a hundred and sixteen lacs drawn directly out of the revenues of Bengal. On the 1st of March, 1780, the Bombay detachment, together with the parties under Camac and others had cost 82 lacs apart from the remittances to Bombay.

The Presidency of Fort St. George complained on 7th December 1778 that the Nabob and the Raja of Tanjore had not fulfilled their engagements. On 30th, while agreeing to the necessity of taking Mahe, they declared that the extraordinary expenses were more than they could bear. A remittance of 10 lacs was despatched to them. Again when their situation became more critical, they called upon Bengal for money. At the time of actual invasion, their funds were wholly reduced. When Sir Eyre Coote arrived at Madras, he at once wrote to Calcutta that the expenses of the expedition would exceed seven lacs a month and every couri (shell) must come from Bengal for "I find there are no resources here from which a single pagoda is expected." The Council of Madras had recourse to the advice of taking up money on bonds upon Bengal, holding as an inducement, the great security of property in that province.

As to the Presidency of Bombay, the Supreme Council had taken upon itself the direction of the war, as well as the necessary supply of troops and treasure for it. Early in 1780 the burden of the war became intolerable. Mr. Francis remarked that the Bombay people had dreamt too long of the inexhaustible wealth of Bengal and had embarked on most dangerous schemes. The currency of the province could not in any degree endure a continuance of the vast drain which had been made upon it by Bombay, and Fort St. George. The Board wrote to Goddard, recommending him to observe the strictest economy, as their resources were no longer equal to the payment of his army. The Bombay Presidency were alarmed. Their treasury was empty. The President then proposed to sell a large quantity of copper as he believed that the rich Brahmans who had deposited their gold and silver in Bombay, for greater security, since the beginning of the troubles in the Marhatta Empire, would gladly exchange it for copper which was also regarded by them as a precious metal.

The General wrote very sympathetically about their distress and declared that he had been compelled to draw bills at a considerable loss for the mere subsistence of the troops. Even that resource was inadequate. The pay of the army was greatly in arrears and the soldiers could no longer be depended on. It is not without interest to learn of the condition of Raghoba. His allowance was stopped by orders from Calcutta and he was reduced to extreme poverty and distress. He had to offer his jewellery for sale in the market and after some time again found himself destitute. He again solicited the general for aid, "The merchants" says Goddard "refused to buy his jewels except at a third of their market value. He said that he was unable to furnish necessary subsistence for his family and did not know what to do under the trying circumstances." Goddard was much embarrassed. Feelings of humanity were added to political necessity; as Nana and Scindhia were hard at work to ingratiate themselves with Raghoba. He therefore granted him an allowance of 10 thousand a month and applied to the Supreme Council but not without a reprimand for deviating from their directions.

The third resource was Loans. In August 1780, another unexpected disaster happened. Charmichael, paymaster general of the military establishment got hold of 9 lacs of Rs: and suddenly left by a ship bound for the Mallacas. The culprit could not be pursued on account of the troubles in the Carnatic. In September, Sir Eyre Coote took up the Governor General's proposal for borrowing money at interest. He said that Bengal, the spring from which all the resources flowed, was exhausted and in danger. It was an urgent necessity that the treasury should be opened to receive money at interest. Besides the pecuniary relief which the scheme would afford, he argued "It would bind as many of the community as possible in our welfare and success by inducing them to place as much of their property as they could under the security of our Govt. It will divest them of the means which in case of an invasion might be used for our destruction." Before Hastings determined upon the final measures, the Council had borrowed every Rupee in Bengal. The distress was extreme. The public funds had been exhausted; but the public necessities increased daily. In November, when it was found absolutely necessary to send a considerable supply of money to Sir Eyre Coote, the Council could not complete the sum from the treasury and had to borrow 5 lacs upon the credit of an influential resident of Calcutta. The pay of the army in Bengal was in arrears. The Oudh army had been in arrears of pay for six months. The Cawnpore Brigade was in the same plight. In January 1781, the Council informed the Court of Directors, of the alarming state of affairs. "We have been reduced to the necessity of borrowing money at interest, by which we have raised Rupees 64,44,601-1-6. This resource cannot last. It must cease but the general exigency which called it forth will continue." Without money the troops would have mutinied. Had not strenuous efforts been made, India would have been lost to the English for ever.

Hastings' extortions.

Under these circumstances, Hastings resolved to force the tributary chiefs to contribute what they could to the needs of the Government. It is significant to note how calmly he set out on the performance of the task which was made the principal charge against him. In a letter dated 28th April 1781, he writes thus: "Lucknow. This head will comprehend money. It is my intention to visit Lucknow. I may set about the beginning of August, and shall travel partly by water and partly by land. I dread the thought of it, for I see infinite need of reformation in that quarter and am afraid, I shall want both time and materials and a vigorous hand to support what I may have accomplished. Something too will be required at Benares and something more than I shall dare to attempt, for if it were left to my option, I would restore that Zemindari to the Nobob of Oudh. Either that ought to be done or the Raja reduced to the condition of a Zemindar." The cases of Raja Cheyt Singh and the Begums of Oudh are not to be treated as individual instances of injustice and violence. They were the natural outcome of a policy which had been persistently followed and with which no body ever found a fault. Violence was used when the British demands were resisted or not complied with. Had there been no resistence, as had been the case on many previous occasions, the conduct of Hastings would have been judged quite differently. The views of the Supreme Council are clearly laid down in the reply, they sent to Fort St. George. The Madras Council, after Haider had overrun the Carnatic, complained that the Raja of Tanjore and the Nobob had afforded them no pecuniary help and had even refused to contribute to the store of grain for the subsistence of the army. We have read" wrote the Supreme Council "with equal surprise and indignation, the representation you have made to us of the disinclination manifested by the Nobob and the Raja of Tanjore, to afford the aids which you have desired of them for the conduct of the war in which they are more immediately concerned than the Company. A case like this will justify you in demanding from the Nobob, the immediate transfer of the whole country in exclusive assignment for the expenses of the war. Such a measure is indispensible in our opinion. We earnestly advise it and had we authority to command, we peremptorily command it". "If such is our opinion" they go on "with respect to the claims of your Government on the Nabob, with much more reason will it apply to the Raja of Tanjore whom we are sorry to see in a state to refuse what any other power standing in the same relation to him as you do, would have taken the wealth and produce of a country which he holds by no sovereign right and must lose whenever your protection is withdrawn from it."

The line of policy thus recommended by the Supreme Council was successful in the Carnatic. The Nabob despatched two agents, Asophudowla and Richard Sullivan to Calcutta and agreed to conclude a fresh treaty which provided for the transfer of the Carnatic to the Company in order to enable them to find resources for the war.

The same reasoning applied with double force to the cases of Raja Cheyt Singh and the Nabob of Oudh. Here the Supreme Council itself were to carry out the policy and it ought to be attended with still greater success. The trouble arose because Raja Cheyt Singh, unlike the Nabob of the Carnatic, did not yield. In July 1779, the Governor-General had proposed that Raja Cheyt Singh should share the burden of the war by paying a subsidy of 5 lacs. Cheyt Singh urged his inability to comply with the demand; but being threatened with physical violence, he paid the amount. In June 1780, the demand was repeated and in November following, it was made a permanent charge as long as the war lasted. The Raja made excuses and delayed. The Governor General could not brook the evasion of his orders, and so determined to visit Benares in person and punish the offence.

The case of the Nabob of Oudh was quite otherwise. He possessed neither intellect nor will. In 1780, his debts to the Company had increased to an enormous sum of 136, 62,188. In December 1779 he had complained of his inability to bear the expenses of the army; upon which the Council told him that the Marhattas were up in arms and any reduction in the army would encourage them to attack his dominions. As the exigencies of war increased, the Governor Gen. and Council pressed their demands upon him and asked him to reduce his public and private expenses. The Nabob submitted and said in reply, "I have never failed in compliance with the Company's pleasure. For your friendship I have cut down the expenses of my table and stopped the Jageers of my aumils. I was at first opposed to assigning Jageers to my grandmother, mother and uncle." In November 1780, the New Resident Mr. Middleton settled the matters with the Nabob who gave assignments to the value of Rs. 98, 98, 375 and for the remainder Rs. 43,18,613 wrote two bonds at 12 per cent interest. The Resident himself bore testimony to the truth of the Nobob's statements. "I sincerly believe them" he wrote "to be the utmost extent of what the Vizir can really grant, by reason of the deplorable state to which the heavy claims of the late years have reduced his finances, rendered more insupportable by the great drain of bullion from these provinces. The great draught of the last year diminishing the rosources while the demands were larger than ever, left him in the most cruel distress, nearly destitute of the means of subsistence and in fact reduced to the necessity of living upon the bounty of his dependants." The Supreme Council insisted on getting the whole of the balance, upon which the Nabob wrote pathetically, "The business of the world is easy and passes away. The Gentlemen of the Council should, in everything that is just, be my guardians and friends. I do not put my life in competition with their friendship. Whatever assets were in my country, with even my table, my animals, and Jageers of my servants and attendants, all are guaranteed in assignments amounting to 98,98,375. Besides these, the Jageers of my grandmother, mother and uncle are at your disposal. I have no other means, for I have no subsistence." The debts increased. The next year the Nabob owed to the Company again nearly one crore. He had no funds, all his resources were exhausted. The Bengal Govt. were in need of money. The Nabob's grandmother and mother, known as the Begums of Oudh to whom reference was made in his letters, were known to possess a large treasury. The Nabob met the Governor General at Benares and secretly agreed to get the money out of their possession. "Whether the seizure" said Scott in defence of Hastings "of 55 lacs was justifiable on the plea of necessity, or whether it is to be defended on other grounds, of this I am certain,and everyone who knows anything of India,thinks with me, that 55 lacs were not to be procured by any other means; and that without such a seasonable supply, we might at this moment be debating how Mr.Hastings should be impeached for losing India. Without money the Empire was lost."

The Impeachment.

These two cases of extortion of money were made the principal charges against Hastings. Our sketch will therefore remain incomplete without a brief examintion of the impeachment. Taking the question in a general way we ought to keep two things in view. The one is, that the contemporaries of Hastings were never able to understand the situation in which he was placed during his career in India. He was the head of a Govt: whose territory and revenue were greater than those of the larger Kingdoms of Europe. Before the days of steam and electricity when it took nearly a year to receive instructions from home on any important matter, he could not depend on the central authority for instructions at all times. The Indian Chiefs and Princes by whom he was surrounded and with whom he had to deal every moment, were all despotic rulers and acted as such. Hastings too in order to be an efficient ruler, had to imitate his neighbours. This necessity led him into a position which from the strictly legal point of view he had no right to assume. The pressure of circumstances made it essential for him to act with absolute authority, if he acted at all. He did what was possible under the circumstances and some of his acts would no doubt be called unjust and iniquitous. But he was guided by that necessity which knows no law. If we once understand that the position of Hastings was that of a monarch and not that of a legally constituted subordinate official, we shall find that the case of his accusers loses much of its strength. Secondly, when we look at the charges more closely, we find that it is not Hastings as an individual who is condemned, but the entire system of British administration as it existed in India before Hastings and continued after him. When Burke charged him with being tyrant, robber, and thief, and expressed regret that the language did not furnish terms of sufficient force to mark the magnitude, multitude and atrocity of his crimes, he in fact brought all these charges against the English power in India. "We have declared him" he said himself "to be not only a public robber himself, but the head of a system of robbery, the Captain General of the gang, the chief under whom a whole predatory band was arrayed, disciplined and paid." From this outburst, he soon passed to a general condemnation of the Compaey's rule. "From Mount Imao to Cape Comorin, there was not a single Prince who had come in contact with the Company, who had not been sold; not a single treaty which the Company had made that they have not broken: not a single Prince or State that had trusted to them without being ruined." Again when, Burke denies to Hastings any credit for having established the British Supremacy in India, he condemns the whole system which had been the means of the growth of English power in India. "Did they ever expect" he said "that we meant to compare this man with Tamerlane or Changez Khan. To compare a clerk at a Bureau, a fraudulent bullock contractor with conquerors of the world? We never said he was a tiger and a lion; no, we have said, he was a weasal and a rat." True, Hastings was not the conqueror of the type of Changez Khan or Timur; but he was a conqueror of a different type. No Englishman could act like Changez, but Englishmen could conquer India as Hastings tried to do. It was by following in his footsteps that his successors did finally conquer it.

Lastly turning to the main-ground upon which Burke wanted to impeach Hastings, we see that it requires great boldness on the part of one to pronounce a judgment on the conduct of Hastings. The standard by which Hastings was to be judged, was in the words of Burke "the Law of God." "Law is the security" he said "for the people of England; it is the security of the people of India; it is the security of every person that is governed and of every person that governs. There is but one law for all, namely that which governs all laws, the Law of the Creator, the law of humanity, of equity, the law of nature and of nations." This was the hardest test that could be applied in the case of any great man of action. If we employ this test to scrutiny the leading events in the history of the world we shall be surprised fo find how much of what is deemed greatness and glory in war, commerce or politics, can be traced to impure sources. The defenders of Hasting's conduct urged the only excuse that the political exigencies might not only suspend but supersede the execution of justice. His advocate Scott said that dominion was easily preserved by the same means through which it was gained. Surely the political morality of Europe in the 18th century was not a bit above the standard which Hastings observed in his actions when every thing which tended to the greatness and security of a soverign's power, was held permissible for him.

The Political Morality of Europe

The nations made war upon each other with the avowed object of territorial aggrandisement and commercial advantage, and "before the fierceness of these appetites," observes a great writer, "the rights of the nations, of races, and even of humanity itself weighed not a feather in the balance." The great Mohammeden historian of the period, took a similiar view of the English aggression in India. "They are a race of men" he writes 'who are keen sighted and full of policy and secrecy, but none so much as the Governor himself whose breast is a casket full of inaccessible secrets. This nation which has not its equal in firmness, courage and strength of mind, is as covetous as any other (and indeed where is the man who in the pride of conscious power and victory has not an avidity for conquests especially if the means be ready)". The author of Hastings' memoirs has discussed the question in the preface, and a quotation will not be out of place here. "His actions and motives speak for themselves. Finally there is one great and obvious truth of which no candid enquirer when he sits down to try the moral probity, not of Mr. Hastings alone, but of other Englishmen, by whom the affairs of India have been administered, will ever be forgetful. The whole of our proceedings in Asia, have been from the first and still are grounded upon a moral wrong. We are usurpers there of other men's rights and hold our Empire by the tenure of the sword. For this, neither the nation nor the individuals may be in strict propriety responsible, because the current of events and not their own ambitious plans swept the India Company onwards to the position which they now hold. Now unless the moralist be prepared to contend that an English Governor of India is bound to betray the trust reposed in him, I think he will be very cautious how he condemns the proceedings. For if Mr. Hastings was corrupt it was to advance the interests of England that he practised corruption. If he was venal, she and she alone profited by his venality; if he was rapacious. into the public territory all the fruits of his rapacity went." The question remains, how was it then that the ablest Englishmen and the greatest orators, raised their voice against Hastings. One view is that Francis whose opposition had been changed into bitter hostility towards Hastings, infused all his venom into the mind of Burke and others. At the time, the partisans of Hastings imputed unworthy motives to Burke, and even to Pitt who had voted for the impeachment. The fact however seems to be that Hastings fell a victim to one of the evils of the system of party Govt. in England. It is an irony of fate that the revolt of the American colonies which had helped so much to develope the political situation in India and create troubles for Hastings, was also the indirect cause of his disgrace.

The Underlying Cause.

The Americans were the children of England. England's war against her Colonies was in a sense, an unnatural war. The conflict had very highly coloured the party politics of England. The Whig members openly wished success to the Colonists and rejoiced at their triumphs. The leaders of the opposition were never less patriotic and more cosmopolitan than at the period when the attention of the Parliament was drawn to the mal-administration in India. Judged in the light of the spirit of humanity as opposed to that of nationalism, Hastings appeared a great criminal. All the evils of the British policy in India were fastened upon him and he was chosen to be the victim.

Few historical characters have been more hardly dealt with than Hastings. His services to the cause of his country afford a rare instance of selfless devotion and energy, The selfcontrol and resourcefulness with which he faced all the troubles, and the devotion to the interests of his country which he displayed during his career, unsupported and unencouraged by the acclamations of his countrymen, are virtues which place him high above ordinary mortals.

When he came to the Government, it subsisted on borrowed resources and its powers were unknown beyond the borders of the country which it held in concealed subjection. Hastings raised it to authority and opulence. He was morally certain, he said once, that if the resources of the country were in the hands of a military people and a constant and undivided Government, they would be capable of vast internal improvement and would raise the power that possessed them to the dominion of all India. He believed that he was capable of improving them and applying them for the real and substantial benefit of his country. How hard he had to labour for the performance of the task, is best told in his own words : "The treaty with Raja Ram Pundit was negotiated and concluded in a week. Let this serve as a proof that I am not idle or uselessly employed when I withold myself from private importunity or from public view which I am often compelled to do, and am employed in secret conversation or in listening to volumes of letters read to me by my Moonshi for hours and even days together, while matters of inferior consideration be neglected. In my department, the proper choice consists not so much in what is to be done, as what can with least inconvenience be left undone. And you know, Scott that whenever my work is to be executed that requires a more than common attention or to be guarded by nice collateral provisions, I always make task my own. Few are the moments that I give to relaxation. My amusements are quiet and domestic and they preserve me in temper. health and spirits, by which I have been enabled to go through as great a load of business, with what effort and ability, let others judge." While speaking of himself in another letter, he says, "My name has received no addition of titles; my fortune, of Jageer; nor my person, any decorating of honour. No provision has been assigned me for a domestic surgeon or a chaplain. Neither my constitution nor my religion have been a charge to the Company." "However my superiors or the world may judge" he wrote "of the policy, of the measures which I have unsuccessfully projected, it is impossible to ascribe it to any other motive than a zeal for the interests of my employers and for the aggrndisement of the British nation and dominion." If Hastings, policy was not quite successful at the time, it was because India had not yet become quite destitute of political capacity. It could produce an astute statesman in Nana and a great soldier in Haider. Hastings had however laid the foundations deep and secure and it was an easy task for his successors to erect the superstructure. But for him, the Marhattas would have been the paramount power in India and the way for English advance would have been completely blocked.

Nana & Haider.

Among the adversaries of Hastings, Nana and Haider are the two worthy names that will ever be remembered in Indian history. Nana was a man of extraordinary genius. He had risen from the ranks. Beginning as a writer to the Peshwa, he rose to the highest position in the Marhatta State. He was to the Marhatta Empire what Hastings was to the British dominions. Both had similar aspirations. Both had to contend against similar difficulties. Both were equally energetic, restless and courageous. Both judged the political situation with unerring insight. Both had the true interests of their nations at heart, and both knew in what those interests consisted. When Hastings was engaged in creating domestic dissensions among the Marhattas and 'raising ancient Kingdoms against them,' Nana was busy negotiating alliances with the French, the Portuguese and the Dutch. Nana had to encounter as much opposition from his colleagues as Hastings from the factious members of his Council. It was Nana who controlled Scindhia and Holkar and by his wise policy prevented them from separating their interests from the Empire. "It is needless to tell you" wrote Goddard, "that Nana is the only person who with the name of the ministers stands forth to negotiate on the part of the Peshwa and the Marhatta State." It was through the success of his policy that the advance of the English was stopped. The formation of the great coaltion was his crowning triumph. "To attempt a character of this great statesman" says the Asiatic Annual Register "would be to detail a history of Marhatta politics for the last 25 years, during which he discharged the duties of minister with abilities unequalled. During the long and important period of his administration by the force and energy of his single mind, he held together his vast Empire, composed of members whose interest were as opposite as the most anomolous elements and by the versatility of his genius, the wisdom and firmness and moderation of his Govt:. he excited this mass of incongruities to one mutual and common effort, with that wise and foreseeing policy which strong in its own resources, equally rejects the extremes of confidence and despair. he supplied from the fertility of unexhausted genius, an expedient for every possible event." Such was Balajirao Janardhan, Nana Farnavis, the greatest statesman produced by Maharashtra who preserved the Empire from internal discord and external attack. While the destinies of the Marhatta State were guided by him, it reached the height of its power. The authority of the Marhattas was firmly established in Delhi, the great and ancient capital of India, the seat of dynasties, Kingdoms and Empires. For nearly 20 years, Delhi was under the Marhatta rule.

Haider was the wonderful political and military genius of the age. Unlike Nizamali, the Nizam of Deccan who enjoyed inportance more from the fame of his family than from any of his own claims. Haider had risen from a low rank. Within a short time, he was master of a powerful Kingdom, the revenues of which amounted to more than 3 crores (30 millions) a year. He had wonderful penetration in discriminating the character of the men with whom he dealt. Nana always admired his braveey and genius. Haider was superior to Nana in one respect; he was a man of action, while Nana was not. His capacity and resolution both in peace and in war challenge a comparison with his great contemporary, Frederick the Great of Prussia, and Haider does not lose by the contrast. In 1777, he possessed an army of about one hundred thousand men. His troops were warlike and well-disciplined. The Madras Council, on enquiries being made by the Supreme Council, declared that Haider would be a useful ally in the emergency of a war with the Marhattas, while little could be gained by a closer union with the Nizam.

Sir Hector Munro, while serving as a common soldier in the army tells an interesting story in a letter to his father. The whole letter was filled with the details of the fighting, so by way of apology he added in the end :" By continually talking on the same subject, my head is so filled with it that I can think of nothing else. There are just now six or seven fellows in the tent, very gravely disputing whether Haider is or is not the person, commonly called in Europe the great Mogul."

Hastings.

Hasting's place in the history of the British Empire is quite unique. The final conflict for colonial Empire was fought out between France and England in Asia and America. at the period when Europe was involved in the seven years war. The whole attention ot France had been absorbed in the affairs on the continent. At the end France found that while she had gained no advantage in Europe, she had lost nearly all; she had possessed in other parts of the world. It will for ever be the glory of Pitt that during his Government England laid the foundations of an unrivalled Colonial Empire. England no doubt stood as the first country in Europe and Pitt was the first Englishman in England. Pitt was yet living and not quite twenty years had passed when there came a crisis which affected the magnificent structure he had raised. The Colonies in America revolted. The enemies of England, especially France burning with the desire of avenging herself on the author of her humiliation rejoiced at the opportunity for destroying England's Colonial power, Through age and disease, Pitt had become unfit for the task of supporting the Empire. It was now beyond his power to save it. He died with his last protest on his lips against "the dismemberment of this ancient and noble monarchy." "The English cause" says Lecky "was pronounced by the politicians of Europe to be ruinous. It was generally believed that the severance of the Colonies would be the beginnings of complete decadence of England. The Imperial feeling being roused, England resolved to make great sacrifices against all Europe combined; but inevible happened, America was lost."

In every part of the world except one, Britain had been a loser. The only quarter of the world in which Britain lost nothing was the quarter in which her interests had been committed to the care of Hastings.

England had passed through a perilous crisis. France sent-her agents to India and the British power had to face a serious danger in that country. A crisis arrived with which he, and Hastings alone was competent to deal. "It is not too much to say" says Macaulay "that if Hastings had been taken away from the head of affairs, the years 1780, and 81 would have been as fatal to our power in Asia, as to our power in America."

Printed at the Hindu Mission Press, NEW DELHI,
and Published by Bhai Parmanand.